The Doctrine
of the Church

The Doctrine of the Church

W. A. Criswell

Convention Press
Nashville, Tennessee

About the Author

W. A. Criswell was born in Eldorado, Oklahoma, and grew up in New Mexico. He graduated from Baylor University and Southern Baptist Theological Seminary. Dr. Criswell entered the ministry in 1928 as a student pastor; he has been pastor of First Baptist Church, Dallas, Texas, since 1944.

Dr. Criswell served two years as president of the Southern Baptist Convention. He is the author of about thirty books.

Contents

Three Ways to Study This Book

LARGE-GROUP STUDY

This book can be studied in a large group. These large-group sessions will be more effective if the leader will adapt the small-group study guides for use by a larger group and use the teaching aids in *The Doctrine of the Church Resource Kit* (item 5123-02).

SMALL-GROUP STUDY

Church Training groups or other small groups can study this book by using the directions for leading small-group sessions. These guides are at the end of the text and give directions for five sessions.

INDIVIDUAL STUDY

You can study this book on your own as well as in a group. Carefully work through each chapter, completing each personal learning activity as it appears in the text. You will be introduced to fresh ideas. Take time to consider and to evaluate each one.

Requirements for receiving credit in the Church Study Course for the study of this book are at the end of the text. (*See table of contents.*)

A New Testament church is a local body of baptized believers who are associated by covenant in the faith and fellowship of the gospel.

Introduction

Baptists hold many doctrinal positions that are shared by numerous other Christian groups. Such concepts as the incarnation of Christ, justification by faith, and other cardinal truths are characteristic not only of Baptists but also of a number of other denominational groups. However, when Baptists begin to discuss the doctrine of the church (ecclesiology), few other church groups join them in a unique but thoroughly biblical understanding of the nature and purpose of the church.

The statement adopted by the Southern Baptist Convention in 1963 defines the church as follows:

A New Testament church of the Lord Jesus Christ is a local body of baptized believers who are associated by covenant in the faith and fellowship of the gospel, observing the two ordinances of Christ, committed to His teachings, exercising the gifts, rights, and privileges invested in them by His Word, and seeking to extend the gospel to the ends of the earth.

This church is an autonomous body, operating through democratic processes under the Lordship of Jesus Christ. In such a congregation members are equally responsible. Its Scriptural officers are pastors and deacons.

The New Testament speaks also of the church as the body of Christ which includes all of the redeemed of all the ages.

This book seeks to accomplish two things. First, every attempt is made to magnify the unique Baptist persuasion that the church is always to be a believers' church, an assembly of twice-born individuals who have borne witness to their faith in baptism and have covenanted together to carry out the mandates of the gospel in a local community. Second, a careful examination of the various facets of church life and organization encourages loyalty to the one organization that came from the heart of Jesus.

Chapter 1 of the book examines the church as it exists in its modern setting. Careful attention is focused on the rival claims of those who reject the church and wish to replace it.

Chapter 2 explains the origin of the church. It examines the concept of a people of God in the Old Testament and concludes with the establishment of the New Testament church by Jesus.

Chapter 3 describes the nature of the church. The richness of the biblical metaphors describing the church are examined. Attention is devoted to the question of the membership of the church, and mention is made of the church as it exists in two different spheres.

Chapter 4 examines the mission of the church on earth. Although diversity of functions is present, the major thrust of evangelization and world mission enterprise is primary.

To carry out the prescribed mission of the church, the local assembly must have government and assigned positions of leadership. Chapter 5 details the various forms of church government possible but argues for a congregational form as being more nearly in keeping with the New Testament. The ministers of the church, pastors and deacons, are also discussed.

Chapters 6 and 7 treat the significance of the ordinances of baptism and the Lord's Supper. Historical background that places the various views of the ordinances in perspective is provided. Finally, the New Testament significance of both ordinances is advanced.

Chapter 8 is a brief look at the future of the church. This chapter is important because of the insistence of some that we now live in a post-church era. Victory in world mission endeavor and triumph at the return of Christ are seen as the prophesied destiny of the Lord's church.

This book on the church is neither definitive nor exhaustive. It is an attempt to lay a foundation and stir up the minds of Baptists to a renewed emphasis on the doctrine and function of the church. The views expressed grow naturally out of the documents of the New Testament and out of the experience of one who has been a pastor for more than fifty years. The book comes to your hand accompanied by the prayer of this pastor that it will be a benediction to your soul and an inspiration to your life.

Chapter 1

The Church Today

Sunday's sunrise is accompanied by the ringing of thousands of alarm clocks across America. Churchgoers prepare to gather just as their fathers have done for two hundred years. By noon, a significant number of Americans from Maine to California have participated in one of a variety of spiritual exercises. Will Rogers once quipped that highway engineers in Texas constructed roads for Texas Baptists to wear out going to and from church.

Even though decline in spiritual awareness in our own era somewhat nullifies Will Rogers' conclusion, surely there is still a worldwide consciousness of religious and spiritual needs. Throughout the world, religious faith remains a viable influence against all inroads of secularism and materialism. Statistical tables in *The Quarterly Review*, July-August-September 1979, establish the religious dedication of the whole human family.

More than 13,000,000 Southern Baptists from more than 35,000 churches contributed $1,869,701,706, of which $316,919,377 was used in missionary efforts. However, the world that Baptists encounter through missions is already intensely religious. Nearly 133,000,000 Americans hold membership in one of 274 diverse denominational bodies. Two and one-half billion people in the world claim connection with some religious faith. Almost one billion of these claim the Christian faith in some form. Another one billion are Moslems and Hindus.

In the midst of this, Baptist work has expanded to every habitable continent and to most nations of our world. The world Baptist family now catalogs 140,118 churches with 33,730,874 members in 112 nations. Whether one evaluates the world psychologically, sociologically, politically, or religiously, religion in general cannot be ignored, nor can the church be specifically bypassed. What is this strange multifaceted assembly of people known as the church? What is its history, and how is its purpose reckoned?

A NINETEEN-HUNDRED-YEAR PHENOMENON

The church was founded by Jesus himself over nineteen hundred years ago. Since that time, the church has suffered internal turmoil, insufferable persecution, misunderstanding, and, in some cases, serious moral and spiritual setbacks. Nonetheless, the church has endured exactly as Jesus promised (Matt. 16:18). In fact, the Lord's people have not chosen a passive and indifferent existence, but have lived militantly and often triumphantly across the years. During this time certain things have been characteristic of the church.

Division

The Lord apparently knew that divisions would occur in the church. His priestly prayer in John 17 was partially a prayer for unity (John 17:20-21). Within a few years of our Lord's ascension, the early church faced the difficulty of deciding whether Gentiles should be admitted to the Jewish-Christian ranks. Predictably, the early Christians were divided on the issue. Subsequent years polarized the issues until the contention became so severe that Paul wrote his forthright letter to the churches in Galatia, insisting that keeping the Law had nothing to do with God's program of salvation.

As centuries passed, controversies about the person of Christ rocked and divided the church. The Protestant Reformation triggered the modern age of denominationalism. Today there are a few major denominational groups and many lesser known and smaller denominational bodies, and they all claim unique insight and emphasis. One would suppose that such splintering would render the church inoperative, or at the least ineffective and unconvincing.

Such divisions have not always been helpful. They have caused suspicion and even failure on numerous occasions. However, God has worked marvelously and effectively among his people regardless of the splintering of the Christian faith. This is illustrated by the way God blessed Paul and Barnabas after their intense debate and eventual separation. Most people recognize that neither God nor Jesus is responsible for the splintering of the church. Splintering occurs because of our human inability to understand all that we should about God.

Dilution
The witness of the church also has been subject to dilution. This has occurred because of encroaching worldliness, mushrooming materialism, and overemphasizing one doctrine to the radical exclusion of others. Worldliness and materialism are always devastating. However, dilution from improper doctrinal balance often occurs because of a reaction to some other weakness in a church.

The church most likely to have a large segment of its membership enamored with the gift of tongues is the church that has been cold, formal, and lifeless. Dissatisfied members searching for something vital and significant sometimes discover a new concept, and they emphasize this new insight until it is entirely out of proportion.

Satan is never at rest. Long ago he learned that he could inflict more severe injury to the witness of Christ by diluting the Christian message than he ever could by persecution and hardship. Therefore, he wages a continued assault on the church of God, attempting to neutralize her witness by diluting her message. Note the enormous growth of the cults, including the inroads of Eastern religions in America. In effect, Satan is saying, "Be religious; just do not cast your lot with New Testament Christianity."

Declarations
If the church of Jesus has been wounded by division and dilution, the wound is not unto death. Southern Baptists alone support more than 5,000 missionaries who are located around the world. Southern Baptists will provide nearly $30,000,000 in support of a Bold Mission Thrust program designed to confront all of the world's population with the claims of Christ.

Such statistics are not the best indexes to the condition of the church. However, they do provide a strong hint that the churches are still profoundly committed to sharing the good news about salvation in Jesus Christ. Seminaries operated by the Southern Baptist Convention are filled with mission volunteers and future pastors. New churches are springing to life all over the United States and Canada. God's people continue to demonstrate their determination to spread the unsearchable riches of Christ until all men have the opportunity to enjoy that spiritual wealth.

Triumph

The church awaits her ultimate triumph when she will be gloriously transformed. But even today the church of Jesus continues to march triumphantly. Billy Graham has preached to more people than any other preacher in history. With the aid of communication satellites, the church has disseminated the gospel in song and sermon to the recesses of the world. Powerful radio signals penetrate iron, steel, and bamboo curtains with the message of the love of Christ.

In our own Southern Baptist denomination, churches have continued to increase the rate of their missionary giving. In lands such as Korea, Nagaland, and Brazil, Baptist work prospers and gives every indication of unprecedented growth in the decade ahead. A healthy confidence in what God is doing in these difficult days sets people apart from the despair so characteristic of the modern era.

PERSONAL LEARNING ACTIVITY 1
A. You have studied four predominant characteristics of the church. List these from memory. Then write two or three sentences about each characteristic, explaining it in your own words.

B. In spite of the difficulties faced by the church, at least four factors have contributed to her continued viability. These factors will be discussed in the following section. As you read, underline key ideas.

THE VIABILITY OF THE CHURCH

What factors account for this spirit of militancy and triumph in many of our churches? How is the church to remain a living reality in a century of dismay and secularism?

A Perpetual Hunger for God

The prophet Amos envisioned a day when the land of Israel would experience an excruciating famine, not a famine of food but of the Word of God (Amos 8:11). The psalmist spoke of panting for God as a deer pants for water (Ps. 42:1-2). Even in an age of reigning secularism, men find themselves with an insatiable thirst for the refreshing rivers of the Word of God.

The obstetrician can deliver new life to the world, but the church nurtures and sustains that life spiritually and provides parents with hope and optimism about the future. The coroner can establish officially the time of death, but only God's people with the life-giving Word can bring comfort. A justice of the peace may perform weddings, but only in the church will a couple learn God's way for a happy and fruitful home.

The crisis situations of life and the inevitable periods of boredom and depression create an unrelenting desire to hear what God has to say. An army of Sunday School teachers and a troop of preacher-prophets in a network of local churches is still viable and essential because people are still hungry for a more certain word from the Lord.

The Arresting Nature of the Scriptures

A person does not have to be hungry for the Word of God to find himself confronted with the claims of Christ. In the congregation that I serve in Dallas, there is a host of Jewish Christians who are a continual encouragement and blessing to me. Many of them sit together just to my left while I am preaching. As I think about them, I often am reminded of the arresting nature of the Word of God. Few of them were seeking the Messiah, and not one had visions about becoming a Baptist. But the Word of God is powerful, like a sword piercing to the depths of our souls (Heb. 4:12). As long as the Word of God is in the world, it will give life to the church because of its arresting nature.

The Permeating Nature of the Church in the Community
Can you imagine a community with all of the churches silenced and closed? Who would stand for morality and righteousness in the community? Who would comfort the distressed? Who would minister the word of the Lord? Such a situation is unthinkable. The cities and the rural areas of our country are sprinkled with churches. Like so many aspects of our lives, the presence of churches is so commonplace that they go unnoticed by us. Churches were the launching pads for most of the early American colleges and universities. Denominationally founded and operated hospitals care for thousands every year. Social injustices often have been righted at the insistence of churches. Churches are woven integrally into the fabric of every community.

The Heroism of Its Adherents
Heroism is not limited to the church or to the religiously inclined. However, a remarkably sacrificial nature has surfaced frequently because of the eternal consequences of the message of Christ and the strategic importance the church attaches to love.

Frequently, that heroism has been exhibited in the midst of persecution. Balthasar Hübmaier and Michael Sattler were early Anabaptists who were burned in Europe for their faith. Felix Manz was immersed until dead in the Limmat River in Switzerland. Bill Wallace remained in China during our modern era only to die at the hands of brutal and godless men. Others simply burned themselves out for Christ through their tireless labors. Lottie Moon died aboard ship in a Japanese harbor while waiting passage home. She had sacrificed marriage, comfort, and probable length of life to witness for Christ in China. Adoniram Judson clung to life and sanity in a vermin-filled Burmese dungeon to finish translating the New Testament into the Burmese language.

Such acts are common to every era of Christian history. They inspire confidence. Men find themselves wishing to imitate such strength. Great causes for which to live and perhaps even to die are rare today. When such a cause arises and its nature is righteous and noble, its followers guarantee its ability to exist.

PERSONAL LEARNING ACTIVITY 2
Without looking back, recall the four factors that have contributed to the viability of the church. List at least two key ideas you underlined under each factor. If you have difficulty doing this, review the section you have just studied.

AN ASSAULT BY RIVAL CLAIMS

Temporary victories, past glories, and the Savior's promise of ultimate victory do not ensure an unhurried and uncomplicated existence for the church; nor do they imply that unyielding foes are not arrayed against her continually. Frequently, churches find themselves immersed in sorrow and strife, suffering from insufficient vision and hampered by the opposition of Satan and the world. There are numerous enemies; and some of the more devastating enemies of the present era are the demonic influence of the cults, the stranglehold of materialism, the reign of humanistic philosophies, and the rapid rise of parachurch organizations.

The Cults

Promising inner peace through disciplined contemplation, the Eastern faiths such as Zen, Hinduism, and others have appealed especially to the young. Years ago, Rudolf Otto noted the importance of the element of mystery in the appeal of any religion. The mysterious, that which transcends the realm of the purely physical, is a major emphasis in the chants and mantras of the Eastern faiths.

Mormonism, Armstrongism, Christian Science, and the Jehovah's Witnesses continue to entice members away from the evangelical faiths. Although these cults are diverse, they all teach an inadequate view of Jesus. Christian Science views Christ as less than fully man, and the other three regard Jesus as less than the eternal God. Obviously, a mistake about the most fundamental axiom of the Christian faith calls into question the right of these cults to be called Christian in the genuine sense.

However, the aggressiveness of these groups in their proselytizing makes them a formidable force opposing evangelical influence.

Some of the difficulty arises from the confusion caused by rival claims to revelation. Mormons and Christian Scientists claim to have additional books of revelation other than the Bible, and the Jehovah's Witnesses have produced their own translation of some of the Scriptures. Furthermore, the actual theological posture of these faiths is often ill-defined and ambiguous. Nevertheless, some find these options appealing and reject genuine Christianity simply because the churches have failed in evangelization and in the clear explanation of Christian truth.

Materialism

In some respects materialism takes a more devastating toll than the pseudo-Christian cults. Blessed with abundance, most Americans enjoy more leisuretime than ever. Transportation is more readily available, and the time required to move from one place to another has decreased. The result of this mobility is that on the weekend, the American public shifts from city to the lake, or to the homes of relatives, or to some other distant point. And people seldom attend church when they are away from home. Harvard theologian Harvey Cox noted years ago that modern life could have as its symbols the cloverleaf highway and the telephone switchboard. The highway emphasizes the mobility of the present age; the telephone stresses the desire to remain anonymous. Both are consequences of materialism.

However, materialism can be just as dangerous within the church as without. Churches often become culturally conditioned, captured by one economic strata, unable to minister to any other. Churches may become so enmeshed in building programs that the object of the ministry becomes the needs of the particular church. The great missionary enterprise, which ought to occupy the hearts of churchmen, is abandoned in favor of monies frivolously spent on increasingly elaborate church social affairs.

Also, increased luxury gives rise to complacency. A person can forget what it is to be in want when he is isolated from

H. Armstrong Roberts

The mobility of today's society presents a challenge that the church may not be able to meet with its traditional approaches.

economically deprived people and areas. Having a myriad of conveniences and the money to buy almost anything one desires makes it increasingly easy to be "at ease in Zion," unconcerned about the plight of the world's sufferers.

Humanistic Philosophy

The inroads of a view that fails to assess adequately the depravity of man pose another threat to today's church. A noted person recently claimed to be a Christian and at the same time said that he believed in the innate goodness of the American people. Although that statement is a typical perception, it reveals a fundamental misconception. Although the Bible teaches that man is fallen and essentially evil, humanism argues for the essential goodness and progress of a human family. Almost without exception, humanism also carries the baggage of evolution with it. Man is not the special creation of God but is the evolutionary result of space plus time plus chance.

Although hope occasionally flickers, multitudes believe that sufficient teamwork among scientists, sociologists, and psychologists eventually will figure out the best answers to man's dilemma, leading to utopian conditions. Such ideas are in perpetual and irresolvable conflict with the claims of the Bible. Humanism is stealthy, clever, and convincing; and as such, it is the enduring enemy of the Lord's church.

Parachurch Organizations

A routine search of the New Testament fails to produce evidence that any agency other than the church is commissioned by Jesus to do the work of the kingdom. But the modern era has produced a growing number of organizations that are not associated with any specific local church but claim to be arms of the church. These groups normally center around special interest groups—athletes, businessmen, college students, and so on. They are generally evangelical in tone; they cross denominational lines; and they claim that they have no desire to become bogged down in minor theological disputes.

Although we should be grateful to God for every person won through parachurch ministries, several important points should be noted carefully.

- There is no real authorization for such groups in the New Testament.
- Such organizations are parachurch, that is, "beside the church." Most often they do not assist the churches significantly. Association with a parachurch organization results too often in little more than requests for money.
- The church by its nature is committed to minister to people from all races, cultures, economic potentials, and positions. Special interest groups are out of place in the church.
- Energies siphoned away from the local church and expended in parachurch organizations would be employed more effectively through the local church, the avenue ordained by God for the work of God.

PERSONAL LEARNING ACTIVITY 3
In your opinion, which of the rival claims has had the greatest effect on your church? List reasons you think that particular rival claim has had the greatest effect on your church.

CONCLUSION
If the church is to counter successfully the assaults of the cults, materialism, and humanism and is to remain militant and triumphant in this age, God's people must recognize the nature and work prescribed for the church by the New Testament. The remaining chapters deal with that role.

FOR FURTHER STUDY
If you feel a need for further study in some of the areas dealt with in this chapter, you will find the following Equipping Center modules to be excellent for individual study or for group study.
The Baptist Way: How We Are Different
The Bible Speaks to Current Issues
The Christian Confronting the Cults

Chapter 2

The Origin of the Church

The church as we know it today was founded by Christ, and his teaching about what the church was to be and what it was to do made it a radical departure for the religious structures of the day. However, it was not a radical departure from the Scriptures. Much of what Christ taught about the church was based on concepts rooted in the Old Testament and on his teachings about persons and their relationship to God.

THE CHURCH IN THE OLD TESTAMENT

From the beginning, God intended to prepare a people especially for himself. Just as Christ, the eternal Son of God, was always in relation to the Father, so God always planned for Christians to be called the body of Christ and to be prepared to be the bride of Christ. The church as we know it today did not exist in the Old Testament. The Old Testament uses figures of speech and types to express God's ultimate plans for the church; and people in the days of the Old Testament awaited the coming Messiah who would create the church.

God's Purpose in a People

On several occasions in the days of the Old Testament, God chose persons or groups of persons for a special relationship with himself; and he made covenants with them.

PERSONAL LEARNING ACTIVITY 4
Study the following covenants and try to identify the elements in those covenants that are also characteristic of God's relationship with the church.

God's covenant with Adam (Gen. 3:21-24)
God's covenant with Noah and his sons (Gen. 9:1-17)
God's covenant with Abraham and his descendants
  (Gen. 12:1-3; 15:18)
God's covenant with Moses and Israel (Ex. 19:5-6)
God's covenant with David and his descendants
  (2 Sam. 7:5-16; 1 Chron. 17:4-14)

These covenants contain elements that are a foreshadowing of the New Testament church. In each, God called a people to himself and bound himself into a relationship with them for the purpose of exercising his righteous rule over them. Yet in none of these covenants did God establish the close, personal relationship that leads to the New Testament description of the church as the body of Christ and his bride.

It is a common mistake to regard the nation of Israel as the church of the Old Testament. In this view, the church is regarded as having begun with the selection of Abraham from among the peoples of the earth to make him and his descendants a special people of God. This line of argument can be defended well on the ground of the New Testament designation of the church as the New Israel (see Rom. 9:6-8; Heb. 8:8-13, quoted in part from Jer. 31:31-34). The major problem with this line of interpretation is that it is backward. As Paul so carefully explained in Romans 11, the Israelites are not cut off from God's promises; but in the mercy of God, they will be called back into their rightful inheritance.

The church stands upon the foundation of Israel's relationship to God. The mission of Christ and the message of the church are inseparably bound up in the Old Testament revelation of God's purpose and plan of redemption. The church is the heir of new promises and of a new covenant into which Israel has never entered. The line of separation between Israel and the church is the event of Christ—his life, death, resurrection, and exaltation before God.

God's Choice of Israel

When we say that the church stands on the foundation of Israel's relationship to God, we mean that there are both ethical and typological connections between the Israel of the Old Testament and the church of the New Testament.

PERSONAL LEARNING ACTIVITY 5
Leviticus 20—21; Hosea 6; and Amos 5 contain ethical requirements that God placed on Israel. Yet these requirements speak equally to the church today. Study these chapters and identify those ethical requirements. Locate in the New Testament passages that state the same or similar ethical requirements.

The Levitical code underscores the requirement for all of God's people of all ages: "Ye shall be holy unto me: for I the Lord am holy, and have severed you from other people, that ye should be mine" (Lev. 20:26). Inherent in Israel's freedom from bondage were ethical requirements; and those requirements carried a promise of spiritual blessing (Lev. 26:3-13). Moreover, when the prophets of Israel called for repentance and return to the right relationship with God, the language they used was ethical language that instructs the church. For example, "I desired mercy, and not sacrifice; and the knowledge of God more than burnt offerings" (Hos. 6:6), and, "Let judgment run down as waters, and righteousness as a mighty stream" (Amos 5:24).

The church is an heir to the ethical instruction of the Old Testament. The difference is that we have the additional interpretation our Lord Jesus Christ gave those instructions. This is an interpretation that Israel did not have.

The apostles of the earliest church of the New Testament saw the church as an heir to some of the prophetic promises (see Acts 2:17-21; Joel 2:28-32), but they also recognized the church as a new creation of God under a new and better covenant than Israel's. The Bible of the earliest New Testament church was the Old Testament. The church of the New Testament stands in ethical continuity with the Israel of the Old, but the church is the new creation of God under the new covenant (Heb. 8:13; 9:15; 12:24; 2 Cor. 3:6). The church continued to take seriously the Old Testament revelation of God, particularly as that revelation pertained to the coming and mission of Jesus Christ, the Messiah.

THE KINGDOM OF GOD AND THE CHURCH

According to Matthew and Mark, the initial message of Jesus' preaching was a call to repentance on the ground that the kingdom of God was at hand (Matt. 4:17; Mark 1:14-15). The kingdom of God is a foundational concept in the teaching ministry of Jesus. Because of the importance of the concept of an understanding of Jesus' ministry and because of the many misconceptions about what the kingdom is and is not, we need to look at the meaning of the kingdom of God in relation to the origin of the church. The kingdom of God in the teaching of Jesus is both a present reality and a hoped-for future consummation. Jesus' announcement that the kingdom of God was at hand meant that the reign of God had broken into human history. "At hand" cannot mean that God's reign drew near in Jesus' day and was removed because the Jews rejected Jesus. A kingdom implies an activity of reigning, a people over whom the reign is exercised, and a realm in which the reign is effective. As we examine these concepts, bear in mind that the concept of a kingdom also implies a King, whom we take to be God himself.

The Reign of God

Part of the present reality of the kingdom of God is his activity of reigning or ruling. The preaching of Jesus makes it clear that God's rule brings two major results: repentance and salvation. In Matthew and Mark, repentance was the primary burden of Jesus' preaching as was that of John the Baptist. To repent is to change the mind, which in turn changes the conduct. Repentance is the change that sees the former state of mind and conduct as wrong and sees the rightness of a new relationship to God. The people to whom Jesus preached his message were in a wrong relationship to God and thus did not allow God to exercise his reign in their lives. Jesus offered them the opportunity to place themselves under God's rule. In the modern world, also, mankind is estranged from God and is in desperate danger of condemnation. The modern message of repentance is a similar offer to allow persons to change their minds about themselves and to place themselves under the rule of God.

God's activity of reigning not only calls for a change of heart in his subjects; it also offers salvation. In salvation God does three things. He sets aside the condemnation that results from wrong action and attitude; he forgives sins and removes sin's penalty, which we so richly deserve; and he includes the person in the permanent kingdom of God. Salvation heals the breach of separation between man and God, pays the penalty of sin, and releases from the power of sin. Jesus demonstrated this saving power as he healed the sick, exorcised demons, and raised the dead. Thus, he showed that the kingdom of God has broken the dominion of wickedness to release persons individually from the power of sin to the reign of God. Not only does Jesus release us from the power of sin and bring us into the reign of God, he also motivates us to continue to live under the reign of God and teaches us how to do so.

The People of God

Jesus' preaching of the kingdom of God refers to God's people gathering voluntarily under God's rule. The church is the earthly manifestation of the kingdom of God. At the same time, we recognize that the church by no means exhausts the meaning of the kingdom of God. The kingdom of God and the church are by no means identical, but the kingdom of God is unmistakably a collection of persons who willingly have submitted to God's reign in their lives.

Fellowship is the common element between the kingdom of God and the church. Both are characterized as a fellowship created by God's activity of ruling. To both, God has brought repentance and salvation; and both are joined together by their common relationship as the subjects of God's kingship.

God's Ultimate Triumph

The third major aspect of the kingdom of God that Jesus announced is an eternal reign or rule by God. This aspect of the kingdom has not yet been fulfilled, and it creates a tension in our understanding of the kingdom of God. The fact that the church is a fellowship of persons redeemed by the saving activity of God's rule points to a future, perfect consummation of the reign of God in an eternal kingdom of God. The present church with its fellowship, worship, and aggressive proclamation is a part of God's activity of ruling and, thus, is a part of the kingdom of God. But neither the church as we see it today nor the church of the New Testament is the perfect institution that will be the consummation of God's reign.

PERSONAL LEARNING ACTIVITY 6

As a review, try explaining in your own words how the kingdom of God is a foundational concept in what Jesus taught about the church. If you have difficulty doing this, review the section you have just studied.

Then before studying further, match each term in the left column with the term in the right column that best matches it.

Discipling   the church's authority

Apostles   the church's endowment

Pentecost   the church's initial human agents

Scripture   the church's commission

The final kingdom that we anticipate includes at least two phases: the end time and the eternal reign of God after all enemies of God have been put under the feet of Christ. That future kingdom will far outshine anything the human imagination may contrive. This marvelous kingdom is the basis of our hope and the goal of our labors in this world. Its relationship to the present church is that the church is a part of that glorious kingdom, just as we who are redeemed by the saving rule of God are part of the church. In some mysterious way there will be a continuity between the temporal church of today and the eternal kingdom of which we shall finally be a part. That continuity and connection are the hope and goal of the Christian life, as they were at the beginning of the life of the church. From the time of its creation, the church has looked ahead to the fulfillment of the promises of Jesus and to our participation in the glorious reign of our Lord.

JESUS AND THE CHURCH
When Jesus came into the world, there existed no such entity as the church. During the years of his ministry, he was laying the foundation for the church and bringing it into being. Ten days after his ascension the church was growing and functioning. It follows that the church began to function between those times. Jesus promised to build his church (Matt. 16:18), so we believe that he did just as he said he would.

Jesus Christ as Founder and Foundation of the Church
Jesus established and built his church for a specific purpose. That purpose is found in the Great Commission (Matt. 28:19-20). The Great Commission is the command of the risen Lord Jesus Christ—marching orders for his church. As such, it deserves careful attention and is the subject of much literature.

The central idea of the Great Commission is the command to make disciples (*matheteusate*, Greek) of all nations. The tense suggests that although the action of making disciples was not then in progress, it was ordered to begin and that making a disciple is a once-for-all event. The term is poorly translated *teach* in the King James Version of the Bible. It meant to the earliest church that the converts were to be brought under the

THE FIRST BAPTIST CHURCH
Founded by Roger Williams A.D. 1638
The Oldest Baptist Church in America

The church as we know it today did not exist in Jesus' day; but it has grown upon the foundation he laid.

same kind of learning discipline as they themselves had been under. The converts were to become followers, learners, and servants of the Lord; they were not merely to absorb doctrine.

The term translated *go ye* in the King James Version is not technically an order. A better translation probably would be *going* or *as you go*. The term states the absolute prerequisite for carrying out the order to make disciples. No disciples could be made until the early church reached outside itself by going to those who needed the salvation offered in Christ. The commission to make disciples carried with it a necessary obligation to go back and forth over the earth carrying the good news that Jesus Christ has brought redemption from sin.

The region covered by the Great Commission is the entire world. The church was assigned the task of winning the whole world to Jesus. This unlimited commission was and is a challenge of the highest order. It is an impossible goal made possible by the life and the gifts given the church through the Holy Spirit. That commission made the church responsible for every person on earth in every generation. The command given by the Lord on his own unlimited authority was to bring all persons under his discipline and rule. He also stated that the two components of that primary task are teaching and baptizing. The converts were to be taught to do everything Jesus taught his own disciples during his earthly ministry. Not a word or an action was to be left out. They were to be instructed so thoroughly that they could in turn instruct other converts.

New converts were to be baptized in the name of the triune God, showing how God has revealed himself to us: (1) Father, Creator, and Sustainer of the universe and of his creatures in particular; (2) Son, Redeemer, and glorified Intercessor for his own before the Father; (3) Holy Spirit, God with us, and Giver of gifts for the building up and unification of the church. It remained for later interpreters such as Paul to explain fully the significance of baptism for the early church (Rom. 6:4; Col. 2:12). The primary significance to the earliest church was expressed in the Great Commission; baptism was an act of obedience to the Lord's command.

The basis for the command of the Great Commission was twofold. (1) " 'All authority in heaven and on earth has been given to me' " (Matt. 28:18, RSV) and (2) " 'I am with you always' " (Matt. 28:20, RSV). Jesus' statement that all authority had been given to him indicates the unlimited resources that were to be put into fulfilling the Great Commission. The order was never intended to be carried out in a half-hearted manner by those who had some time on their hands. It was the primary commission and marching order of the church. The authority of Jesus Christ would command the emptying of the coffers of heaven and the impoverishment of earth if necessary to procure every soul for whom Christ died. The promise of Jesus' continuing presence indicates that the church was not commanded to go alone but to depend on the resources her Lord would provide. The church was to take comfort in the knowledge that her Lord was always to be in the struggle for the souls of mankind. No promise could be sweeter nor authority more compelling than this beautiful commission.

Having been constituted, endowed with a fellowship, given her two ordinances, and given her permanent orders, the church was fully established at the ascension of Jesus. Yet the church was not in operation at that time. One more thing was needed to make the church functional.

The Disciples as Human Agents in Extending the Church
Jesus personally called the church into being by calling to himself a group of disciples. Although by the time of Pentecost the group of disciples included many more than the twelve, it was the twelve who were the primary hearers of all Jesus' teaching and the primary witnesses of all Jesus' miraculous signs showing the power of the kingdom of God. When they were called and the group was formed, they were called disciples. A disciple was a follower, a learner, and a servant, according to the custom of the time of Jesus. They formed a close group around their Lord, going with him in all his traveling ministry. They left their homes, their trades, and their families to be close to Jesus. They were entirely dependent on Jesus and on one another for their food, shelter, clothing, and spiritual growth. Jesus saw to all these needs with the primary emphasis on spiritual growth.

The disciples were learners. They sat, listened, and apparently memorized great blocks of material from Jesus' teachings. The

Gospels are clear that they did not understand all that they learned. Nevertheless, they learned; and they had faith that they would come to understand in God's time.

One of the concepts the disciples learned by repetition was that they were never to abandon their servant status. The first-century disciple was a servant of his teacher, but such disciples often became arrogant, overbearing masters. The disciples of Jesus learned that their Master remained a servant and came to serve all mankind. Since the servant cannot rise above the Master, they understood finally that they, too, were to be servants of God in Christ.

The groupings of the names given in the lists of disciples in the various Gospel accounts indicate that there were circles of special friendship within the overall circle of fellowship among Jesus' followers. The disciples may have included as many as three pairs of brothers: Peter and Andrew, James and John, and possibly Matthew (Levi) and James the son of Alphaeus (see Matt. 4:18,21; Mark 2:14; 3:18). The names of the disciples are listed in Matthew 10:2-4; Mark 3:16-19; Luke 6:14-16; and Acts 1:13. A comparison of these lists indicates that the first pair of brothers was close to the second pair. Philip and Bartholomew are mentioned together in the Gospels. Matthew and Thomas are also mentioned together in the Gospels. In Acts the order is Philip and Thomas, Bartholomew and Matthew. Thus, these four may have been a close group. Three more disciples are always mentioned together; James the son of Alphaeus, Thaddaeus (Judas), and Simon the Zealot. When Judas Iscariot is mentioned, he is mentioned last; and the only time he is connected with another disciple in a list is in the Lukan list where he is joined to Judas the son of James (Thaddaeus). Likely, the lesser James, Thaddaeus, and the lesser Simon were also relatively close friends.

The designations for the disciples' inner circle in Mark and in Acts constitute a remarkable independent verification of the unity of the group. Mark, referring to the time before the events of Jesus' suffering and death, refers to the close disciples as the Twelve. Acts, referring to the time after the ascension of Jesus, calls this same group, less Judas Iscariot, the Eleven. This group, more than any other people, enjoyed fellowship with Jesus.

After the ascension, their unity continued as a fellowship of those who had been with Jesus throughout his ministry. This fellowship was a major part of the earliest church.

Pentecost as Endowment for the Church

Having been commanded to await the coming of the Holy Spirit in Jerusalem, the incipient church assembled in an upper room and held a prayer meeting for about ten days. This was the time between Jesus' ascension (about forty days after the Jewish Passover) and the coming of the Jewish feast of Pentecost (fifty days after Passover). Although the church was fully constituted, it was not yet functional because it had no power. On the day of Pentecost the power came. That power was the Holy Spirit, who breathed life into the church and filled the individuals who composed it. The fact that about three thousand converts were added to the church that day (Acts 2:41) shows that the church began to function immediately when it received the Holy Spirit.

The church Jesus founded during his earthly ministry had waited to be brought to life. It was a potential church before Pentecost. The members were amazed by the events of the preceding months. They knew intellectually some of the things that had happened, but they had not appropriated the power and the authority Jesus had conferred on them. They had not yet received the Holy Spirit.

Although the prophet Joel had foretold the pouring out of the Holy Spirit, the experience at Pentecost was a new thing in Israel (Joel 2:28-32). Old Testament heroes of the faith had received the Holy Spirit for a time, but the Holy Spirit came at Pentecost to dwell among mankind forever. It was the Holy Spirit who gave life to the church Christ built. This life was evident in the power that the church exhibited. Under the influences of the Holy Spirit, all the believers spoke about Jesus Christ and salvation. The power of the Holy Spirit was so effective that it even undid the curse of Babel, the confusion of languages, to allow the communication of the good news about Christ. Moreover, Simon Peter, who had caved in before the questions of a servant girl, stood before the crowd to proclaim boldly the message and witness of the Lord.

Surely no power on earth could have made this frightened

collection of leaderless people into the bold witnesses who changed the history of the world. Only God could have done it; and it was their testimony that he had. The gift of God that empowered the early church was the Holy Spirit—God choosing to make himself present with his redeemed people.

PERSONAL LEARNING ACTIVITY 7
The gifts of the Holy Spirit were given to the members of the early church individually. And they were given for a specific purpose. Study Romans 12:3-8; 1 Corinthians 12:4-11; and Ephesians 4:1-16 and write a brief statement explaining what that purpose is.

The gifts of the Holy Spirit were given to the members of the early church individually. However, the purpose of the gifts was not to enlighten the individuals to whom they were given. There is no indication that the earliest church ever understood this to be the purpose of the gifts. Rather, the gifts of the Holy Spirit to the primitive church were specifically to enable persons to bear witness to the good news about Jesus Christ to the end that those who were lost might be saved. These gifts were always to glorify Christ and to unify and build up the church (Rom. 12:3-8; 1 Cor. 12:4-11; Eph. 4:1-16).

The Scriptures as Authority for the Church
The writers of the New Testament made frequent use of the Old Testament as a source of authority for the church and for the Christian life. Not only did they quote the Old Testament as authoritative, they used the ideas and persons of the Old Testament as examples of how the church was to function and how the Christian was to act. When quoting the Old Testament, the New Testament writers frequently introduced such material by using such words as, "It is written." This statement almost always translates a Greek expression that could be expanded in English to this: "It stands written with continuing authority."

This usage indicates the high regard of the New Testament authors for the Old Testament revelation.

Jesus set the example for this high regard for the Old Testament by using three quotations from Deuteronomy to ward off the temptations of Satan in the wilderness (Matt. 4:4,7,10 from Deut. 8:3; 6:16; 6:13, respectively). Jesus used the Old Testament to explain his mission and ministry (Luke 24:27) and his use of parables in teaching (Matt. 13:11-15; Mark 4:11-12; Luke 8:10).

Jesus also set the stage for the preparation of the New Testament with his promise of the Holy Spirit as One who would teach the disciples all things and bring all things back into their memory (John 14:26). On this basis the inspired apostles under the guidance of the Holy Spirit prepared a number of manuscripts for the direction of the church.

The New Testament books were written, then, under the guidance of the Holy Spirit for the benefit for the church. These books even suggest that they were written so the church would be built up and unified: "So that you might know the exact truth about the things you have been taught" (Luke 1:4, NASB). "But these have been written that you may believe that Jesus is the Christ, the Son of God; and that believing you may have life in His name" (John 20:31, NASB). "He appointed some to be apostles, others to be prophets, others to be evangelists, others to be pastors and teachers. He did this to prepare all God's people for the work of Christian service, in order to build up the body of Christ. And so we shall all come together to that oneness in our faith and in our knowledge of the Son of God; we shall become mature people, reaching to the very height of Christ's full stature" (Eph. 4:11-13, GNB). "All Scripture is inspired by God and profitable for teaching, for reproof, for correction, for training in righteousness" (2 Tim. 3:16, NASB). "Let us be concerned for one another, to help one another to show love and to do good. Let us not give up the habit of meeting together, as some are doing. Instead, let us encourage one another all the more, since you see that the Day of the Lord is coming nearer" (Heb. 10:24-25, GNB).

Toward the end of the apostolic period, the early church began to realize that the apostolic writings were the foundation on which future development of the church would depend. Some of these writings apparently were intended by the authors for general use; for example, the Gospels, Acts, Hebrews, James, 1 and 2 Peter, and Revelation. Others, such as most of the Pauline epistles, apparently were written in response to some problem or definite need in a particular person or church. The earliest copies of a few of the Pauline epistles even bear evidence that some of these letters were used as circular letters after their initial purpose was accomplished. The earliest church apparently understood the need for the collection of the New Testament soon after the completion of the apostolic period. This collection under the guidance of the Holy Spirit came to be the third foundation of the church following the apostles and the commission.

PERSONAL LEARNING ACTIVITY 8
You should now be able to tell if you completed correctly the last half of personal learning activity 7. If you have any doubts about the correctness of your work, you should review the material that follows the learning activity.

CONCLUSION

When Christ said that he would build his church, he meant what he said. He did it himself, personally. When he returned to heaven, he left a church in the world. At Pentecost the Holy Spirit breathed into that church the breath of life, and she became a living soul. After God made Adam, he breathed into him the breath of life. In the valley of dried bones in Ezekiel, the breath of God had to make the dead stand up and live. Before Christ left, he called the body he left behind in the earth a church.

The Nature of the Church

Hardly a day passes without a visitor from somewhere coming by to see the premises of the First Baptist Church in Dallas. When asked what they do with a camera focused at the historic building, the common reply is, "I'm taking a picture of the church."

Of course, that is a common notion about the church. Many people normally associate the term *church* with a building, as does the dictionary. Others use the word to designate a state church, as in "the Church of England." Still others call a denomination a church as in "the Lutheran Church." Although these are common usages, none is consistent with the meaning of the term *church*. Neither is there scriptural support for any of those uses. What is the church? Several descriptive terms will help us understand.

DESCRIPTIVE TERMINOLOGY

The New Testament uses several terms and figures to describe the church. Five of those are considered here.

PERSONAL LEARNING ACTIVITY 9
The following section is a study of five terms used in the New Testament to describe the church. As you study each term, study carefully all the Scripture references in the text. Then complete the appropriate section of the chart on pages 42-43.

Ekklesia

Our English term *church* comes from the Scottish word *kirk* and the German *kirche*, both derived from the Greek *kuriakon*. *Kuriakon*, and thus *church*, is definitely an appropriate name since it means "that which belongs to the Lord (kurios—Lord)." But *ecclesiastical* and *ecclesiology* are derivations from the Greek *ekklesia*, the most common word translated *church* in the New Testament.

Ekklesia is composed of two words: *ek*, meaning *out of*, and *kaleo, to call*. The main idea of being called out is not so much that of being separate and exclusive as it is that of a purposeful assembly. People were called out of their homes and summoned to meet for a specific purpose.

In the Septuagint (the Greek translation of the Hebrew Old Testament), the Old Testament usage of *ekklesia* has no particular religious significance. It simply means a gathering, that is, a gathering of evildoers (Ps. 26:5), of an army (Ezek. 32:22-32), of military officers (1 Chron. 13:1-2), and even of the whole nation of Israel (Josh. 8:35). But to be part of the *ekklesia*, one needs to be physically present.

Although the same basic meaning is dominant in the New Testament, the Holy Spirit gave the word additional meaning. Some examples show a nontechnical use—that of a gathering. Acts 7:38 refers to Israel's gathering in the wilderness (see Heb. 2:12). There are some usages that resemble the technical sense but not quite as precisely (1 Thess. 1:1; 2:14; 2 Thess. 1:1,4). The verses do not designate a specifically Christian assembly. The use of *ekklesia* to designate a physical assembly that is distinctively Christian by virtue of spiritual unity is used in Acts 11:22; 13:1; and 1 Corinthians 1:2.

Some cases also depict a figurative, not physical, *ekklesia*. Spiritual unity is stressed and the church is not relegated to one specific locality. Such is the concept of the universal church (Acts 9:31; Gal. 1:13; Phil. 3:6). In Matthew 16:18, Jesus could not have meant a local institution but *ekklesia* in the generic, qualitative sense. In Hebrews 12:23 the assembly is linked to Christ, the Firstborn among brethren (Rom. 8:29). The members of the assembly are citizens of the heavenly as well as of the earthly spheres.

Ekklesia, therefore, is that body of people spiritually united by the common experience of faith in Jesus Christ (the universal sense, as Matt. 16:18 and 1 Cor. 12:13) and physically united in assemblies at various times and places (the local sense, that is, the churches of the New Testament).

The Bride of Christ

Marriage is a figure used to depict the relationship between God and the nation Israel in the Old Testament. "Thy Maker is thine husband; . . . . For the Lord hath called thee as a woman [wife]" (Isa. 54:5-6). The New Testament also describes the church as the bride of Christ (Eph. 5:22-32; Rev. 21:9).

There are at least two predominant teachings in the idea that the church is the bride of Christ. (1) Christ (the figurative husband) is the head of the church (the figurative wife). Although human husbands and wives are essentially equal, God has assigned the husband the functional responsibility of leading and caring for the wife. As by God's design the husband is the head of the wife, so is Christ the head of the church (Eph. 5:23). (2) As Christ, who is the head, loved the church to the point of laying down his life for her, so is the husband enjoined to love his wife even to the point of laying down his life for her (Eph. 5:25). An additional expectation from a husband who loves is that he looks after the welfare of the wife ("nourishes and cherishes") as does Christ of the church (Eph. 5:29).

The imagery is intended to impress us that Christ is genuinely interested in and actively involved in the affairs of the church. Anyone who treats the church out of ill motives should remember what Christ said to Saul on the road to Damascus: "Why persecutest thou me?" Any self-respecting husband expects others to respect his wife. Thus, Christ expects respect for the bride whom he loves. As we shall see in chapter 8, the church is the bride being kept and made ready to be united with the Bridegroom in the imminent future.

The Body of Christ

The human body is God's awe-inspiring creation. The term *body of Christ* is used to describe another aspect of the church. Unlike the other figures for the church, this one does not have

Biblical Terms That Describe the Church

EKKLESIA

In my own words, this term means:

This aspect of the church is important to me because:

BRIDE OF CHRIST

In my own words, this term means:

This aspect of the church is important to me because:

BODY OF CHRIST
In my own words, this term means:

This aspect of the church is important to me because:

FELLOWSHIP OF THE SPIRIT
In my own words, this term means:

This aspect of the church is important to me because:

KINGDOM OF PRIESTS
In my own words, this term means:

This aspect of the church is important to me because:

an Old Testament precedent. Yet this appears to have been Paul's favorite analogy (Rom. 12:15; 1 Cor. 10:16-19; 12:12-27; Eph. 1:23; 2:16; 4:4,12,16; 5:23,30; Col. 1:18,24; 2:19; 3:15). Note that the church is the body of Christ and not just of Christians. There is a mystical union between Christ and the church; that is, the church as a corporate body is in reality, though intangibly, the body of Christ. We are part of Christ so that we are known as being in Christ (2 Cor. 5:17).

As the human body has the metabolism for life and growth, it also has the limbs and organs necessary for the body to be able to function. The same is true of the church. God has given each person spiritual gifts and talents and abilities that are needed by the church. For the church to function with maximum effectiveness, it is essential that each person use his gifts, talents, and abilities for the good of the body. By God's design, not even the smallest or most insignificant part of the body is unessential. This is true of both the universal and the local church. Each person in the body of Christ has been put there by God and has been given spiritual gifts, talents, and abilities that are essential

---

PERSONAL LEARNING ACTIVITY 10
A. Complete the following statement: I am important to my church because

B. Write a paragraph explaining why you think some other member of your church is important to the church. Write or call that person to tell him why you think he is important to the church.

---

to the life of the total body. It is impossible for a person to live normally without one arm or one eye or three fingers, as it is for the body of Christ to function unless each of its parts is functioning properly. "The eye cannot say unto the hand, I have no need of thee: . . . . God hath tempered the body together, . . . that the members should have the same care one for another" (1 Cor. 12:21-25).

Although God gives persons various responsibilities in the church, only Christ is designated the Head of the church (Col. 1:18). Christ as the Head is the sole source of leadership, direction, and life. Even pastors are under the Head; they are under-shepherds of the Shepherd. Christ, the Head, needs no representative. Whenever two or three are gathered in his name, he is in their midst (Matt. 18:20). Is it not comforting to know that Christ is present in our worship and prayer services as well as in our business meetings? The head controls all the parts of the body and enables them to function together. Christ is the Head of the body, the church.

The Fellowship of the Spirit

The New Testament uses two words, *koinonia* and *metoche,* to describe the deep relationship that exists among Christians as they work together to fulfill the mission of the church. The major prerequisites of fellowship are likeness of nature (2 Pet. 1:4) and community of purpose (Heb. 3:1). Furthermore, each Christian has been brought by the Holy Spirit into the life of the body, the church (1 Cor. 12:13). Apart from this, there is no fellowship of the Spirit. Their citizenship is in heaven (Phil. 3:20), and they are fellow pilgrims and strangers in the world (1 Pet. 2:11). Because God is their Father, Christians experience discipline (Heb. 12:8); but they are also heirs of future glory (2 Cor. 1:7; 1 Pet. 5:1).

Because of these common experiences (Jude 3), members of the church are known by their mutual love and concern for one another (John 13:34; 15:12). When one is burdened, the other shares the load (Gal. 6:2). A weaker brother is upheld by a stronger brother (Rom. 14; 1 Cor. 8). They hold the same fundamental doctrines ("common faith," Titus 1:4; Eph. 4:3-6) and see to their preservation.

Because of the inherent nature of the fellowship, a Christian is commanded not to be yoked with unbelievers (2 Cor. 6:14-16) or participate in unfruitful and unedifying works of darkness (Eph. 5:11). A Christian cannot say he is in fellowship with God and at the same time lack the demonstration of love for a brother (1 John 2:9-11).

Perhaps the most neglected element of fellowship is the possibility of its denial to some. Our Anabaptist forefathers called this action "the ban." It is known in church circles as church discipline and is clearly taught in 1 Corinthians 5 and 2 Corinthians 2:4-11. Flagrant offenses, that is, immorality, deserve public censure (1 Cor. 5:1-4), and consequently fellowship is cut off. Uncooperative spirit and disdain for responsibility are also worthy of discipline (2 Thess. 3:6-15). The purpose for all discipline is the correction, the instruction, and the encouragement of obedience and faithfulness on the part of the church member. Although fellowship demands discipline in the sense of separation, it demands nonetheless the imminent restoration of the offender.

A Kingdom of Priests

Despite the diversity in gifts and functions, the church is one body, and all its members have the same relationship to Christ. Access to God's presence was once the exclusive privilige of priests. It still is. But the change is that believers are made priests unto God and enjoy direct access through Christ's death and resurrection (Rom. 5:1-2; Rev. 1:5-6) so that priesthood now includes all believers. The reformers Luther, Calvin, and Zwingli challenged the Roman Catholic Church on this crucial doctrine. Baptists have traditionally upheld the position that the reformers took.

Peter called the church "an holy priesthood" whose responsibility is no longer that of slaying and offering animals but of offering "spiritual sacrifices, acceptable to God by Jesus Christ" (1 Pet. 2:5). Paul said we should offer our bodies as living sacrifices (Rom. 12:1-2), and the writer to the Hebrews commanded that spiritual offerings be made with lips full of thankful praises to God (Heb. 13:15).

The belief that every believer is a priest is functional in Baptist worship services, church government, and ministry. One is asked to "lead the congregation in prayer"; thus, the congregation prays for all the requests. As many members as possible participate in the services, and the whole congregation normally sings and reads the Bible together as an act of corporate worship.

In contrast with the episcopalian and presbyterian forms of church government, the congregational form is used in Baptist churches to enhance our belief in the priesthood of every believer. Every member shares in the formulation of policies for the local church so that it is not subject to the authority of any external body. The church is autonomous; that is, it rules itself. It voluntarily aligns itself with associations of like convictions, while guarding the right not to be ruled by external bodies.

Because every member is a priest unto God, he is equipped by the Holy Spirit with a gift or gifts to minister and to contribute to the fulfillment of the church's mission (Rom. 12; 1 Cor. 12; Eph. 4:11-16). The goal of all the employment of gifts is the mutual edification of the body so that, in turn, the body could reach out and evangelize and disciple all within reach of a church's influence.

PERSONAL LEARNING ACTIVITY 11
Baptists state two requirements for membership in a local church. Before you study the next section, try to state these two requirements and give the reasons for each.

THE MEMBERSHIP OF A CHURCH

A man or a woman is not a husband or a wife apart from a commitment of life through the institution of marriage. A person is not a soldier apart from a commitment to his country by enlistment in the armed forces. By the very nature of being a Christian, it is inconceivable for one to be a follower of Christ apart from personal membership in a church.

Regeneration

People can enroll in institutions and apply for membership in organizations. But not so with the church. One becomes a member of a family by being born into it or by being adopted into it. A Christian is both born into and adopted into the family of God. Like Nicodemus, a man needs to be "born again" or more precisely, "born from above" (John 3:3-18). Christian parents do not bear children who are automatically Christian. Becoming a Christian is a birth brought about only by the Spirit of God. This is what is known theologically as regeneration.

Regeneration is the inner recreating of fallen human nature into a new nature. When a person confesses Christ as Savior and Lord and receives him into his life, the Holy Spirit transforms that person's life (Titus 3:5; Rom. 12:2). By virtue of that transformation, a new man emerges (Eph. 4:24; Col. 3:10). If any man be in Christ, he is a new creature. The old nature ceases to be in control; the new life has begun (2 Cor. 5:17). This is the reality which we are commanded to keep in mind and which we should keep putting into practice (Rom. 6:3-11). Through the renewing work of the Holy Spirit and by the instrumentality of the Word of God (Eph. 5:26), a person is born into the family of God. This is our ground for calling God "Father" (Rom. 8:14-15), and it is the first requirement for church membership.

Baptism

Being born into the family of God is portrayed concretely by a public identification with that family. That public identification is baptism. The significance of the ceremony and the mode by which it is administered is described in Romans 6. It is important, however, to note that baptism is an act that follows the experience of regeneration. Baptism is not the means or the cause of regeneration.

What is the relationship of baptism to church membership? All believers have experienced spiritual baptism, that is, every believer has been spiritually "immersed" by the Holy Spirit into the body of Christ. That body (the universal or invisible church) is manifested in local assemblies. Because the New Testament stresses the importance of the local assemblies without denying the reality of the universal church, both spiritual and physical baptism are equally valid necessities. Spiritual baptism is necessary for membership in the universal church and physical or water baptism is necessary for membership in a local church. The relationship between baptism and church membership is seen in numerous New Testament examples. At the first gospel preaching after Penetecost, "they that gladly received his word were baptized: and that same day there were added unto them [to the local body at Jerusalem] about three thousand souls" (Acts 2:41).

THE CHURCH IN TWO SPHERES

In addition to the universal (or invisible) and local (or visible) aspects, theologians speak of the church militant and the church triumphant.

Militant Battle in This Age

The church on earth from the day of Pentecost to the return of Christ is called "the church militant." As the name suggests, the church is called to and is actually engaged in spiritual warfare. In his announcement of the founding of the body, the Lord intimated such a reality when he declared that "the gates of hell shall not prevail against it" (Matt. 16:18). Thus, armed with the array of spiritual armor, the body of Christ launches an assault against the powers of darkness (Eph. 6:10-19). She is on the offensive. Although the forces of Satan put up an impressive front at times, they are destined to fall.

For us, this means that when we live the Christian life and seek to fulfill our discipling mission, we are engaged in a spiritual warfare, and we ought to be aware of it. This might be an alarm to you. Wake up! We are at war! The Christian life is not a playground; it is a battleground. Realizing this, we ought to make better use of the whole armor of God and rely on the power of the Holy Spirit in witnessing and in preaching the gospel. Paul asked the Ephesian church to pray for him as he preached the gospel to loose people from the chains of Satan.

An additional aspect of militancy is that of serving the functions of being "the salt of the earth" and "the light of the world" (Matt. 5:13-16). The church's mission is discipling the nations. She must keep this mission primary, else she is bound to die by the loss of her distinctiveness and identity. But the secondary and peripheral aspects of militancy call for engagement in the war against poverty and injustice, in humanitarian movements, and in the positive aspects of politics, ecology, and conservation. The church militant seeks to promote the good and thereby suppress the influence of evil.

Triumphant Victory in the Age to Come

This sphere of the church is better conceived through an illustration. At certain points in the football season, some games are played a day or a few hours before they are telecast. Watching a football team fumble or be intercepted is not disturbing when one knows that the outcome of the game is a victory. Although we are in the heat of the battle, we can take assurance in the fact that victory is ours. We have been given a preview of the final results (Rev. 16—20). This, nonetheless, should encourage us to keep on the offensive and not slack off on our militancy.

Although victory is to be realized fully in the age to come, there are those who have already "laid down their burdens down by the riverside and who ain't gonna study war no more." Recently, a nine-year-old boy gave his heart to Jesus in our church. About a year earlier his father had died suddenly and unexpectedly and tragically. With simplicity of faith, the boy asked me, "Pastor, do you think my father can see me from where he is in heaven today?" It was impossible to hold back the tears in my eyes as I said, "Yes." Hebrews 12:1-2 tells us that "the church triumphant" watches us with interest, as if to encourage in us the will to persevere in the spiritual battle. That cloud of witnesses is the church triumphant. But whether in this age or in the one to come, whether on earth or in heaven, really and truly, the church is triumphant.

THE CHURCHES OF THE NEW TESTAMENT

Jerusalem

With the coming of the Holy Spirit to indwell the disciples, the church, in both its universal and local aspects, was born. Spiritual baptism was first experienced by the one hundred and twenty disciples in Jerusalem on the day of Pentecost, and they constituted the first local assembly (Acts 1—2), to which others were added later (Acts 2:41,47).

The twelve apostles served as the leaders of the newly formed community. Judas Iscariot had been replaced by Matthias (Acts 1:21-26); however, this should not be interpreted as a hint of apostolic succession. In fact, a few years later, Herod Agrippa executed James, the brother of John, and the Scriptures do not record that the vacancy was filled. When help was needed in the physical ministries of the church (Acts 6:1-5), the local body under the sanction of the apostles selected the first seven deacons. (There is sufficient reason to think that the diaconate originated here.)

Believers in Jerusalem were known as followers of the Way (Acts 9:2; 19:9,23; 24:14,22). They, voluntarily and spontaneously, practiced the community of goods, and the funds were administered by the apostles (Acts 4:34-37). To this church, and particularly to Peter, Paul presented himself about the third year after his conversion (Gal. 1:18). Both Barnabas and Silas, Paul's companions in the missionary journeys, were members of the Jerusalem church. Because of intense persecution, the church in Jerusalem reached the extremes of poverty. As a gesture of their concern, the local churches in Galatia, Corinth, Macedonia, and Achaia sent relief to their fellow believers in the mother church (1 Cor. 16:1-3; Rom. 15:25-27). That act shows that although local churches are autonomous, they can and should associate with others of like convictions. Also, the first council or convention of the churches was held at Jerusalem to settle doctrinal and practical disputes (Acts 15).

Antioch

The followers of Christ first received the designation *Christians* in Antioch (Acts 11:26; 26:28; 1 Pet. 4:16). The word is formed from the title *Christos* and the colloquial suffix *ianos*—a suffix borrowed from Latin and used to denote one's slaves or some members of his household, that is, the Latin Caesarianus—the household of Caesar (Phil. 4:22). Thus, a *Christianos* is a servant of Christ or a member of his household. Nicolas, one of the seven "deacons" in Jerusalem, was specified as being from Antioch.

Antioch is most likely the second local church to be organized formally. The church had prophets and teachers named Simeon, Lucius, and Manaen, along with Barnabas and Saul (Acts 13:1-3). From the same record, we discover that the congregation at Antioch was engaged in the activities of a local body and first commissioned Barnabas and Saul for missionary service at the bidding of the Holy Spirit. Another evidence of the function was that of gathering for Jerusalem famine relief, which was taken to the mother church by Barnabas and Saul (Acts 11:27-30). The same men conferred with the leaders of the Jerusalem church—the Lord's brother James, Peter, and John—about the progress of the Gentile mission and about the content of the gospel preaching to the Gentiles. There was the clear intimation of the autonomy of the body at Antioch. But one should not fail to see that the meeting yielded the principle that autonomy does not mean dissociation (Gal. 2:1-10).

There was a Greek Christian from Antioch named Titus at the Jerusalem meeting. Because Titus was a Greek Christian, he was uncircumcised, and it is interesting that no one raised the issue of circumcision and salvation at the conference in Jerusalem. Titus later became one of Paul's trusted colleagues.

Corinth

Economic prosperity and unrestrained sexual immorality characterized the commercial center and port city of Corinth. The temple of Aphrodite endorsed that kind of behavior and gave it a religious aura. The city's notoriety gave the Greek language an unusual verb—*corinthiazesthai*, literally "to corinthianize"—meaning "to corrupt or pervert." Immorality was only one of the numerous problems in the church at Corinth. Yet Paul referred to them as "sanctified in Christ Jesus" and "saints" (1 Cor. 1:2). How unbecoming, one might suppose. But where sin abounded, grace abounded much more.

During his first days in Corinth, Paul visited the synagogue. There he met Aquila and Priscilla, who had been expelled recently from Rome by an edict from Claudius (Acts 18:2). Among the other converts in Corinth were Gaius, Titus, Justus, and Crispus, a ruler of the synagogue and "the household of Stephanas"—all baptized by Paul himself (1 Cor. 1:14-16).

The two letters of Paul addressed to the church in Corinth

PERSONAL LEARNING ACTIVITY 12

Beside each church, write several words that characterize or typify that church. If you have difficulty at any point, review the section and Scripture references you have just studied.

Jerusalem

Antioch

Corinth

Ephesus

Smyrna

Pergamum

Thyatira

Sardis

Philadelphia

Laodicea

reflect the life and ministry of that local body. They disputed about preferences for leaders (1 Cor. 3); they observed the Lord's Supper, although with some disorder (1 Cor. 11); and they disputed about the proper use of gifts in the worship and prayer services (1 Cor. 12—14). Although all these functions are oriented to specific problems, they at least serve to show how a local body had problems, as Corinth did. If any church was a poor testimony for Christ, Corinth was. But Corinth nonetheless was part of that bride whom the Bridegroom intended to present without spot or blemish. Critics of the church ought to take special note of this.

The Seven Churches of the Apocalypse

God's final written revelation to men was addressed to seven local churches in Asia Minor (Rev. 1:4). John knew of those churches and as the map of the first-century Roman Empire shows, the cities where the churches were located form a semicircle and are within a few miles of one another.

Although the churches were seven historical assemblies, God's description of them and prescription for them have universal applications. The characteristics of the seven bodies are remarkably typical of churches in any era. Christ's messages for them, therefore, are applicable to all churches of every age.

Note that each church had an angel or messenger, most probably, the pastor (Rev. 2:1,8,12,18; 3:1,7,14). They were told to exercise discipline (Rev. 2:2,20) and to engage in specific activities commanded for them. Furthermore, each church was promised a specific reward in the age to come.

FOR FURTHER STUDY

If you feel a need for further study in some of the areas dealt with in this chapter, you will find the following Equipping Center modules to be excellent for individual study or for group study.

How to Pray for Others
The Bible Speaks to Personal Crises
The Christian and Divorce
Making Good Marriages Better
Your Family: Learning, Loving, Living
Your Home and Christian Discipline

Chapter 4

The Mission of the Church

God has always had a plan for his people. That plan reached its climax when he sent his Son to seek and to save the lost (Luke 19:10). Jesus understood that his mission was to call sinners to repentance. He came to "preach good tidings unto the meek; . . . to bind up the brokenhearted, . . . to proclaim the acceptable year of the Lord, . . ." (Isa. 61:1-3; Luke 4:18-19). Jesus also came to make disciples who would be able to go out with the good news of God's redemptive work.

He gave this same mission to the church (Matt. 28:18-20): " 'Go therefore and make disciples of all nations, baptizing them in the name of the Father and of the Son and of the Holy Spirit, teaching them to observe all that I have commanded you' " (Matt. 28:19-20, RSV). It is clear from this commission that the mission of the church was and is to be an extension of the ministry of Jesus.

THE REDEMPTIVE MISSION OF CHRIST

From the first glimmer of gospel revelation recorded in Genesis 3:15, God has been declaring his purpose of redemption. The advent of our Lord Jesus was the zenith of that redemptive purpose. When the Word became flesh and tabernacled among men, it was done so that Jesus might give himself a ransom for sinners (Matt. 26:28). Jesus came as the love gift of the Father to redeem those who were in spiritual darkness (John 3:16-18).

The Extent of His Mission

Jesus did not limit his ministry to any ethnic, social, political, or cultural segment of the world community. He was a visible proof that God loved all men everywhere (John 3:16). The New Testament word for *world* is *kosmos*. The word is all-inclusive. It means that the extent of the redemptive work of Jesus is universal in its application.

Such a mission seemed improbable, if not impossible. There were many ethnic, social, religious, economic, cultural, linguistic, geographical, and political barriers that would have to be overcome. The Jewish converts were steeped in a narrow spirit of religious nationalism and pride that had caused them to look down on the non-Jewish nations for centuries. When Jesus showed interest in those who were not Jewish, the Jews could hardly believe that God was really concerned for the salvation of all men everywhere.

Jesus did not share the Jews' narrow nationalistic spirit. He surprised his disciples by deliberately going through Samaria. He shocked them by talking to a woman of questionable character. Because of his compassion and concern, many people of that village came to experience the love of God (John 4:1-42). He stirred the traditionalists by inviting publicans and sinners to follow him (Matt. 9:10-13). He assured his critics that he had come as a physician to those who were spiritually sick. Jesus clearly demonstrated that he was willing to transcend all barriers to meet spiritual needs.

The Distinctiveness of His Mission

The prophets of the Old Testament were reformers. They came calling men to repent and turn to God. John the Baptist was an extension of that aspect of the ministry of the prophets. Jesus began at that same point with a stirring call for men to repent (Matt. 4:17). But there was something more to his preaching than had been in that of the prophets or of John. All his predecessors spoke with the authority given them by God. Their message calling men to change direction and turn to God was, "Thus saith the Lord."

Jesus was not a reformer but a redeemer. He did not come saying, "Thus saith the Lord," but rather with, "I say unto you."

This directness and authority surprised and amazed his hearers (Matt. 7:28-29). He came to do more than merely call men to repentance. He came to be the Redeemer by offering himself as the sacrifice for sin. He did not come to give man the answer to the problem of sin. He came to be the answer (Rom. 6:23).

There is a unique sense of mission and purpose evident in the earthly ministry of Jesus. He was keenly aware that he had been sent on a divine mission by the Father. He knew that the Father had sent him to be the Savior of the world. " 'No one can come to me unless the Father who sent me draws him' " (John 6:44, RSV). Also, Jesus said, " 'I have come down from heaven, not to do my own will, but the will of him who sent me' " (John 6:38, RSV).

Even in the practical application of the ministry of Jesus, there was a special sensitivity and compassion for the needs of others. Undoubtedly, others also saw the suffering and the needs caused by sin; but Jesus was willing to do something about them. He went about healing the sick, restoring sight to the blind, raising the dead, and forgiving men of their sins. He was more than a programmer of the gospel. He practiced it and taught his disciples to go and do likewise.

The Methods of His Mission
Several elements are evident in the methods by which Jesus sought to bring men to the Father. First, Jesus received his careful preparation. Jesus began his public ministry at age thirty. We know little about the years of preparation preceding his public ministry. Luke relates that these were years of well-rounded development mentally, physically, socially, and spiritually. In these years Jesus grew in "wisdom and stature, and in favour with God and man" (Luke 2:41-52).

Second, a sense of priority characterized the mission of Jesus. His methods were motivated by a sense of being about the Father's business (Luke 2:49). In his teachings Jesus gave the disciples a cardinal rule: "Seek ye first the kingdom of God, and his righteousness" (Matt. 6:33).

Third, Jesus went out preaching and teaching the word of God. The Sermon on the Mount, Matthew 5—7, is an excellent example of the proper balance that should characterize good proclamation. Jesus' preaching was the word of God about the coming of the kingdom. His teaching included the practical attitudes and activities that should characterize the kingdom citizen.

Fourth, Jesus' method was personal. He brought salvation to the world, but he ministered to the needs of individuals. The disciples were his pupils. Jesus liked to be with people. He was able to relate to others, whether the person was a woman of Samaria (John 4:1-26) or a rich ruler (Mark 10:17-22). Jesus sought to meet individual needs.

Fifth, Jesus came performing great miracles, which were authenticating signs. Although Jesus' miracles were to meet specific human needs, they also showed without a doubt that the power and favor of God rested upon the Master. The miraculous element was to continue among his disciples in the early days of the New Testament church as a sign of God's favor, blessing, and authority (Acts 15:12).

The methods of Jesus never become obsolete. Compassion, concern, and personal interest are always in order. The miraculous is always a possibility with the people of God. The methods that Jesus employed in his ministry will work just as effectively today. The methods of the Savior do not need modification, only application.

PERSONAL LEARNING ACTIVITY 13
Without looking back, recall the five elements evident in the methods by which Jesus sought to bring men to the Father. If you have difficulty, review the section you have just studied. Then list these five methods down the side of a sheet of paper. Beside each element use two or three sentences to evaluate the strength or weakness of that element in your life.

The Cooperation in His Mission
Jesus was a living illustration of Romans 8:28. God was indeed working all things to the best advantage of our Lord's mission.

There was a beautiful oneness evident in the life of our blessed Lord Jesus in his relationship to the Father and the Holy Spirit (John 14:8-9; 17:11). It was this unity that enabled Jesus to achieve such success in his divine mission. The results produced were by the power of God (Matt. 28:19-20). It was within that cooperation that redemption was accomplished (John 1:40-51), making peace with God available (Phil. 4:2-3).

When disciples put on the mind of Christ, dissension dissolves, and controversy quiets. All become partakers in the promise, " 'Lo, I am with you always, even to the end of the age' " (Matt. 28:20, NASB). Thus, the work of the Holy Spirit is to produce unity and cooperation in the body of Christ. The disciples were a fractured group when they disputed over who would be the greatest in heaven (Matt. 20:20-24). But when they were all filled with the Holy Spirit, they were undefeatable (Acts 4:7-8,13). The key to cooperation among those who make up the body of Christ is unity with the Holy Spirit.

THE FULFILLMENT OF THE MISSION OF CHRIST BY THE CHURCH

The missionary mandate of Matthew 28:18-20 underscores Jesus' intention that the church be an extension of his own earthly ministry. His redemptive work was to be extended into all the world by the preaching of the gospel. The church was sent out with his compassionate concern as her example, his authority as her credentials, and his redeeming grace as her message. The same methods that Jesus employed are the methods that the church is to employ.

PERSONAL LEARNING ACTIVITY 14
The material that follows deals with four activities that the church should engage in to fulfill the mission of Christ. Before you read on, list on a sheet of paper what you think these activities are. When you finish studying this section, check your list and make any necessary corrections.

When the resurrected Jesus appeared to the disciples, he said to them, "Peace be unto you: as my Father hath sent me, even so send I you" (John 20:21). It is obvious that Jesus understood that he was sent by God and that he was in like manner sending his disciples into all the world as an extension of that ministry.

Evangelism

Jesus announced that one of the purposes for which he came was to seek and to save the lost. The good news of salvation was at the heart of his mission. Although the church does not save, she is to offer the message of salvation that Jesus provides.

What exactly is evangelism? Unfortunately, this is a much distorted concept. Many say that evangelism is personal soul-winning or revivals or visitation or outreach. Although it includes all of these, it is actually more than any single activity. Evangelism involves doing what our blessed Savior did. It is placing ourselves completely at his disposal that we may be used by him to confront the world with the message of his salvation. The motive and end of this effort is that people will be led to a personal commitment to the Savior. It is our responsibility to confront, while we are to let the Holy Spirit convict. The church receives the increase.

Jesus came to confront the world with his redeeming grace. The church is to extend that confrontation by proclaiming the gospel to all persons everywhere, by watering the seed when planted (1 Cor. 3:5-10), and by praying for the Lord of the harvest to provide laborers (Matt. 9:38).

The methods of evangelism should be as varied and as imaginative as those that Jesus used. He went out preaching, teaching, healing, and ministering. Yet all that he did was evangelistic. He used every opportunity to make every person aware of his need of a personal relationship with the heavenly Father. He had a sense of urgency that was appropriate for the life and death mission on which he came. This same sense of urgency should be characteristic of our own witness. In the parable of the great supper, Jesus strongly suggested that we are to go out and compel others to come in (Luke 14:23).

Worship

Before the Exile, the Hebrews were committed to the Temple and its centralized worship in Jerusalem. At the time of the Exile and thereafter, worship was associated with their veneration of the Law. Jesus came with a revolutionary concept in worship. Worship is not to be confined to a building, a liturgy, or a Sunday morning program. Worship involves all of life. Worship spills over into every area, all activities, and each interest of one's life (Pss. 84; 105; 122; John 4:20-24).

For years the Jews had been locked in controversy with the Samaritans about the correct place to worship God. The Jews maintained that true worship could be done only in Jerusalem. The Samaritans insisted that true worship could take place only on Mount Gerizim in Samaria. When Jesus met the woman at the well, she asked him about this. Jesus' answer is significant. He said, "The hour cometh, and now is, when the true worshippers shall worship the Father in spirit and in truth" (John 4:23). Then he added, "God is a Spirit: and they that worship him must worship him in spirit and in truth" (John 4:24).

Although the formal program of worship is an important time of fellowship and service to God, worship should not be confined to a sanctuary. It is the mission of the church to teach all men everywhere to worship God at all times and in all places.

Worship is proclaiming the "worth-ship" of God. Nowhere else is that "worth-ship" more clearly seen than in the person of the Lord Jesus Christ. By making disciples of all nations, the church fulfills her responsibility to call persons to the highest act of worship possible, giving one's life in personal commitment to Jesus. Such a commitment should result in effective service faithfully rendered.

Worship out of a committed life, resulting in faithful service, leads to the ultimate glorification of the church (Rev. 4). The twenty-four elders in the vision of John the apostle represent the believers of the Old Testament plus the New Testament church as they are gathered around the throne worshiping the Father and the Lamb. Thus, worship leads to service and finally to the glorification of the believer when Jesus comes to get his bride to dwell with him in eternal splendor.

Teaching

Jesus commanded his followers to go into all the world and make disciples. In the New Testament the Greek word for *disciple* is *mathetes* (literally a *learner*). The command to make disciples in Matthew 28:19 is an imperative form of the same root. By definition, a Christian disciple is a learner of the great principles of faith which Jesus came to teach us. Also, the command tells us that the church is to be a communicator of these truths. The church is under mandate from the Lord to indoctrinate the world with the things of Jesus.

The New Testament church followed this pattern. At the end of his ministry, the apostle Paul instructed Timothy to commit the things that he had learned to faithful men who would be able to teach others also (2 Tim. 2:2). The men that Jesus trained and discipled were the ones who were motivated and empowered by the Holy Spirit to share the good news of the gospel.

The church's teaching ministry is an extension of the ministry of our Lord and is to include all the commands of the Lord (Matt. 28:20). This teaching ministry was to be a work of Christ extended to the disciples in the power of the Holy Spirit (John 16:13-15). Claiming the promise of the Holy Spirit's help, the disciples went from house to house sharing the gospel witness (Acts 20:20).

Jesus was a master teacher. He left a wonderful example for the church to follow in an effective teaching ministry. He taught on his own authority (Matt. 7:28-29). The church can speak with the same authority when it speaks the words of our Lord. Jesus taught out of his personal experiences. He was effective in his teaching about prayer because he practiced prayer. He related his messages to the experiences of his hearers. He took situations from everyday life and used them as illustrations of truth (Matt. 6:5-6). When Jesus taught, it was with a compassionate concern and sincere desire to help others. If the church can go with the message of Christ and with the compassion he showed, the gospel can be proclaimed effectively.

Nurture

The work of the church is not complete with the conversion of the lost and the teaching of the unlearned. Growth is a process. Bringing men to Jesus gives them a new birth. Nurture provides for continued growth and development. Just as it takes many years to progress from infancy to adulthood, spiritual growth goes on after spiritual birth. This process of growth or edification in the lives of Christians is an ongoing responsibility of the church.

Edification involves nurture, growth, and development to maturity. Romans 14:19 says, "Let us therefore follow after the things which make for peace, and things wherewith one may edify another." Edification is a New Testament concept. The word *edify* is from the Greek word *oikodomeo,* which means *to build,* as in building a house (1 Cor. 3:9). The body of Christ is God's building which is nurtured through the word (Acts 20:32), through an attitude of love (1 Cor. 8:1), and through the administration of the authority of Christ in our lives (2 Cor. 10:8).

Edification is made possible through the various gifts that God gives to the members of the body, the church. These gifts are mentioned in Romans 12:6-8; 1 Corinthians 12:1-11,27-31; and Ephesians 4:11-13. In the Ephesians passage, the verses that follow call attention to the fact that the purpose of the gifts is to produce Christians who are well grounded in the faith (Eph. 4:14), growing to maturity (Eph. 4:15), and going out with an evangelistic fervor (Eph. 4:16). The gifts of the body are from God (Eph. 4:7-11), for the good of others (Eph. 4:12), and for the glory of God (Eph. 4:13).

Disciplining her members is an often-neglected aspect of the church's responsibility in the area of nurture. Discipline is important if the church is to accomplish its mission effectively. Through discipline sound doctrine is maintained (Titus 1:13). Disorders and inequities can be dealt with by discipline (2 Thess. 3:6-15). If some remain unrepentant and disobedient to the word and will of God, they are to receive discipline (1 Cor. 5:3-5,13).

Discipline, to be administered successfully, must be carried out with utmost care. It must be administered in meekness (Gal. 6:10), in love (2 Cor. 2:6-8), and in submission to the authority that God places over us (Heb. 13:17).

CONCLUSION

The mission of the church is an extension of the earthly ministry and mission of the blessed Lord Jesus. It is universal in its scope and application. Every believer should possess a unique sense of call to be a part of the mission of the church as it is presented in Matthew 28:18-20 and Acts 1:8.

Although the church is an institution, it must respond to the needs of people on a personal basis. Careful preparation should precede all that the church does. The people of God must share the gospel with enthusiasm and look to Christ to authenticate and support the claims of the Word. The work of the Holy Spirit is essential in accomplishing this task. He enlightens and empowers the church for its mission. Evangelism, effective worship, preaching, and teaching are worthy goals to which the church should commit herself.

FOR FURTHER STUDY

If you feel a need for further study in some of the areas dealt with in this chapter, you will find the following Equipping Center modules to be excellent for individual study or for group study.

God's Bold Plan for Missions
God's Mission/Our Co-mission
Helping a Child Understand Salvation
How to Motivate People
How to Study Your Bible
How to Witness
Training Sunday School Workers in Outreach
Understanding Baptist Beliefs

Chapter 5

The Polity, Ministers, and Leaders of the Church

THE GOVERNMENT OF THE CHURCH

The New Hampshire Confession of Faith, adopted in 1830, was one of the earliest and remains the most important of the Baptist confessions of faith. It formed the basis for many subsequent statements, including the statement of "The Baptist Faith and Message" first adopted by the Southern Baptist Convention in 1925. Article thirteen of the New Hampshire Confession is entitled "The Church." It reads:

[We believe] That a visible Church of Christ is a congregation of baptized believers, associated by covenant in the faith and fellowship of the Gospel; observing the ordinances of Christ; governed by his laws; and exercising the gifts, rights, and privileges invested in them by his word; that its only proper officers are Bishops, or Pastors, and Deacons, whose qualifications, claims, and duties are defined in the Epistles to Timothy and Titus.

Herein lies one of the most distinctive features of Baptist faith—its polity, or form of government.

The Historic Forms of Church Government

Since the first century, a number of different forms of church polity have developed. In general, though, three principal types of church government have been most common in the history of Christianity.

One is the *episcopalian*, coming from the Greek word *episkopos*, which means *bishop* or *overseer*. In this form of government, authority rests with the bishops. These bishops preside over a number of individual churches, and they alone have authority to ordain to the ministry. In many cases, episcopalian bodies argue that there is a succession of function and authority from the apostles to the bishops of the present. Most Catholic and Anglican communions, as well as some others, have an episcopal form of church government.

Another type of church government is the *presbyterian*, coming from the Greek word *presbuteros*, which means *elder* and describes government by a council or presbytery made up of elders. Modern Presbyterian churches practice this type of polity.

A third type of church government is *congregationalism*. In this form of government, authority rests with the membership at large, the congregation. Congregationalism stresses the independence of the local church and the priesthood of the believer. Higher human authority within the church or over the churches is denied, and pastors are regarded as full-time servants—not church managers. Baptists are among those bodies that practice congregational polity.

The New Testament Pattern for Church Government

All of these types of church government can claim some support from the New Testament. We should keep in mind that God has blessed sincere believers of every persuasion through the years. Still, we want to discover, as best we can, the New Testament pattern of church government.

The New Testament does not give detailed instructions about church government. Because we must find the proper pattern in bits and pieces, three notable features of the early church are explained here.

First, churches in the New Testament are represented as local, independent, autonomous bodies of believers. There is no evidence that any outside authority was imposed on the local churches, except by the apostles, whose teaching was binding. As the apostles' doctrine became more widely known and as the apostles themselves began to pass from the scene, the church's autonomy became more apparent. Moreover, except for occasional reference to the church as the body of Christ, that is, all the redeemed, the word *church* is only used in the New Testament for a local assembly. Strictly speaking, there is no such thing as the Baptist Church, only Baptist churches. Not until the third and fourth centuries did churches begin to submit to outside authority and institutional organization.

Second, it is apparent that the government of the local church of the New Testament was in the hands of all the people rather than in the hands of a small group of rulers. Paul addressed his letters to entire congregations (Rom. 1:7; 1 Cor. 1:10), as he did specific instructions about necessary church practices (1 Cor. 11:2) and doctrine (Gal. 3:1-3; 1 Tim. 3:15). Other New Testament writers did the same (1 Pet. 1:1; Jude 3). The whole church bore the responsibility for church government. Although both pastors and deacons had special responsibilities, the assembly was the governing unit.

Third, although the New Testament churches never appeared as part of an organization that could exercise control over them, they did associate with one another. Normally, their cooperation was for benevolent, fraternal, or missions causes (Acts 11:22-26; Rom. 16:3-5; 2 Cor. 9:1-2) but never as a form of government.

The Prominence of the Holy Spirit
The early churches emphasized their independence and autonomy because they clearly recognized the work of the Holy Spirit. The church is an assembly of believers, regenerated (John 3:5-6), indwelt (1 Cor. 6:19; Eph. 1:13-14), and led by the Holy Spirit (Rom. 8:14; 1 Cor. 2:10-11). Every believer is therefore free before God as a priest (1 Pet. 2:5,9). And for that reason, every church is a dwelling place for the Spirit (Eph. 2:21-22; 1 Pet. 2:5), free to follow his direction.

The local New Testament church found its polity in the harmony and unity of Spirit-led believers (Eph. 4:1-3). Indeed, disunity grieves the Spirit (Eph. 4:30-32). The New Testament church is a local body of believers indwelt, led, taught, and empowered by the Holy Spirit. Since the Spirit anoints every believer (1 John 2:20,27), he leads through the whole body, not through a few.

The idea of external human authority over the churches seems out of touch with the New Testament. But we should remember that we are just as out of touch when our emphasis on organization or blind denominational loyalty stifles the free working of the Holy Spirit in our churches.

THE MINISTERS AND LEADERS OF THE CHURCH

The New Testament concept is that every Christian is a minister. The New Testament church is not a Broadway play for which one pays a price to be entertained by professionals. It is an army whose readiness and worthiness depend on well-trained, dedicated soldiers, all of whom perform specific and vital tasks under the able leadership of a commander.

Pastors and other leaders are not appointed to perform the ministry but rather to equip others to perform it. In Ephesians 4:11-12, for example, Paul wrote:

And he [Christ] gave some, apostles; and some, prophets; and some, evangelists; and some, pastors and teachers; for the perfecting of the saints, for the work of the ministry, for the edifying of the body of Christ.

Unfortunately, in verse 12, the King James Version places commas, which make it seem that these who are given gifts by the Lord have three jobs: (1) the perfecting of the saints, (2) the work of the ministry, and (3) the edifying of the body of Christ. However, the Greek text uses three different words (all translated *for*) to connect these three clauses. The correct reading shows that the first clause defines the task of the ministers, the second defines the task of the saints, and the third describes the ultimate goal of the ministry. The Amplified Version has it this way:

His intention was the perfecting and the full equipping of the saints (His consecrated people), [that they should do] the work of ministering toward building up Christ's body (the church).

Maybe we are missing something by not calling our pastors equippers. We err when we fail to recognize this New Testament pattern and to make it a vital reality in our churches.

The Office of Pastor

In the New Testament, three different titles are given to one who is charged with the spiritual leadership of a local church. In Ephesians 4:11, Paul spoke of the pastor (*poimen*). In 1 Timothy 3:1, he listed the qualifications for a bishop (*episkopos*). In Titus 1:5 we read that the apostle left young Titus in Crete to ordain elders (*presbuteros*).

Although many see different offices in these titles, there are at least three compelling reasons for believing that *poimen* (pastor), *episkopos* (bishop), and *presbuteros* (elder) are descriptive names for the same office. Although the words translated *bishop* and *elder* are used more often in the New Testament, the following discussion will use the term *pastor* because it is most familiar to Baptists.

First, other than the names themselves, there is no suggestion in the New Testament that more than one pastoral office ever existed. Paul told Titus, for example, to ordain elders, but he did not mention bishops or pastors. He gave Timothy qualifications for bishops, but not for elders or pastors. In Ephesians 4:11, though other preaching offices are mentioned, we find only one pastoral office, the pastor. If more than one such office existed, the New Testament does not make it clear.

Second, the three terms often are used synonymously and are never distinguished from one another. From Miletus, Paul summoned the elders (*presbuterous*) of the church at Ephesus (Acts 20:17). In his exhortation to them, though, he reminded them that the Holy Spirit has made them overseers (*episkopous*) to feed [*poimainein,* literally to pastor] the church (Acts 20:28). Peter exhorted the elders (*presbuterous*) to "feed [*poimanate,* literally pastor] the flock of God . . . , taking the oversight [*episkopountes,* literally bishoping] thereof" (1 Pet. 5:1-2). Paul gave Titus orders about the appointment of elders (*presbuterous*) in Crete (Titus 1:5). But when he gave the qualifications for an elder, he said, "a bishop [*episkopon*] must be blameless" (Titus 1:7).

Third, whenever the officers of the church are listed formally, invariably there are only two, pastors and deacons. Paul addressed his Philippian letter "to all the saints in Christ Jesus . . . , with the bishops and deacons" (Phil. 1:1). The most comprehensive list of qualifications for church officers mentions only the bishop (1 Tim. 3:1-7) and the deacon (1 Tim. 3:8-13). There is no hint of another office.

Why, then, are three different words used for the office of pastor? Apparently, these are descriptive terms, each of which represents the office in a unique way.

The pastor. The word translated *pastor* is the Greek word *poimen*. As a title, it occurs only once (Eph. 4:11), though it is found frequently in other forms to describe the pastor's work. The word literally means *shepherd*. The ministry of the New Testament pastor is deeply rooted in the soil of ancient Israel.

The land in the Middle East is rocky, barren, and inhospitable. In such an environment, the work of a shepherd is vitally important and enormously rigorous. It was no less so among the ancient Hebrews. In isolation, and often in deprivation, a faithful shepherd led his sheep to grazing lands and water supplies, protected them from the attacks of carnivorous beasts, and guarded against losing sheep that strayed away. Usually, the shepherd was employed by a master who himself owned the sheep.

The shepherd had a unique responsibility; and if he was a good shepherd, he was a remarkable individual. Although he did not own the sheep, he cared for them as though he did, devoting himself completely to them. At the same time he was committed to his master and sought to please him. It is not surprising to learn that our Lord Jesus is sometimes described as a shepherd (John 10:1-18; Heb. 13:20; 1 Pet. 5:4).

The Hebrew shepherd is a beautiful illustration of the pastor's work. The pastor is the shepherd of God's flock. He does not own the flock; but in his devotion to God, he watches over it with tender love. In his tending the flock, he is mindful of three awesome responsibilities that belong to him.

First, he must feed the sheep. That can only mean that the pastor is to feed his people the Word of God. Paul encouraged the Ephesian elders to "feed the church of God" (Acts 20:28), which he related to teaching pure doctrine that can withstand those who will come "speaking perverse things" (see Acts 20:29-32). The apostle reminded Timothy that a bishop must be "apt to teach" (1 Tim. 3:2). Paul also reminded young Timothy that elders who rule well are to be worthy of double honor, "especially they who labour in the word and doctrine" (1 Tim. 5:17). Where the noun *poimen* occurs as a title, it is in conjunction with the word *teachers* (*didaskalous*). In fact, the Greek construction of Ephesians 4:11 suggests that the words *pastor* and *teacher* refer to the same office, the office of pastor-teacher. Like a shepherd, the pastor is to feed the flock.

Second, the pastor is devoted to the protection of the sheep. Like the Palestinian beasts that threatened the Israelites' flocks, spiritual enemies lie in wait for God's people. False teachers and false teachings and the influence of a world given over to sinful desires are only the most obvious. The pastor is to protect the flock from these adversaries (Acts 20:29-31).

Third, the pastor cares for the sheep. The ministry is not an occupation, an avocation. The pastor has committed his life to the people with whom God has charged him. The Savior expounded this principle when he said, "The good shepherd giveth his life for the sheep" (John 10:11). In contrast, "The hireling fleeth [from the wolves that attack], because he is an hireling, and careth not for the sheep" (John 10:13). The pastor must be devoted to the care of his people.

The elder. The most common word for the office of a pastor is *elder* (*presbuteros*). It occurs at least fifteen times in the New Testament.

Basically, *presbuteros* refers to age, that is, *elder* as opposed to *younger*. In both Testaments that fundamental idea gives way to the concept of a leading man, one who has grown wise and honorable as he has grown old. Frequently, the word signifies an officially recognized governmental position. Early in Israel's history Moses appointed *elders* to help him govern the growing nation (compare Ex. 18:13-27; Num. 11:16-17; and Deut. 1:9-16). Elders were recognized leaders in the years of the monarchy (1 Sam. 4:3; 2 Sam. 5:3) and in the years during and after the Exile (Jer. 26:17; Ezra 10:7-8). By the time of

Christ, the eldership was a regular governmental position, and the ruling body of a Jewish community was the council of elders. The Gospels frequently mention Jesus' conflicts with the elders of the people.

When the New Testament writers called the early pastors elders, two ideas were in view, dignity and leadership.

The dignity of the pastor's office is a trust, both for the people of God and for the man of God. God's people are to cultivate a deep respect for the office of the elder and for the man who fills that post. Paul admonished Timothy, for example, to entertain no accusations against an elder without substantial evidence (1 Tim. 5:19). The elder, by virtue of his office, merits a great degree of trust and honor.

There is another side to the esteem in which the people are to hold their pastor. Paul said that it ought to be reflected in his pay. In 1 Timothy 5:17 Paul said, "The elders that rule well [should] be counted worthy of double honour, especially they who labour in the word and doctrine." This double honor is explained in the next verse when the apostle quoted from Deuteronomy 25:4 and the exhortation of the Lord in Luke 10:7: "For the scripture saith, Thou shalt not muzzle the ox that treadeth out the corn. And, The labourer is worthy of his reward" (1 Tim. 5:18). The double honor of the elder is the thoughtful and generous provision for his need.

The dignity of the eldership is a trust that also belongs to the pastor. In 1 Timothy 4:12, Paul apparently had in his mind the ancient use of the word *elder* for an aged man who had grown wise, able, and venerable. All of those qualities of the elder apply to the Christian pastor except one—age. So Paul exhorted young Timothy, "Let no man despise thy youth" (1 Tim. 4:12). A pastor is to be blameless (Titus 1:6-7; 1 Tim. 3:2). His walk should be marked by Christian virtue, both as the avoidance of evil (Titus 1:7; 1 Tim. 3:3), and as a positive love of godliness (Titus 1:8; 1 Tim. 3:2), exemplary family life (Titus 1:6; 1 Tim. 3:4-5), spiritual maturity (Titus 1:9; 1 Tim. 3:6), and an honorable reputation in the world (1 Tim. 3:7).

At this point, it is appropriate to consider the matter of a pastor's marital background. The oft-debated instruction of Paul in Titus and in 1 Timothy is that the pastor must be "the

Clyde Denton Jr.

The pastor should be committed to the care of his people; and the people should hold the pastor in deep respect.

husband of one wife" (Titus 1:6; 1 Tim. 3:2). All arguments usually boil down to one of two alternatives. Either Paul was warning against polygamy (more than one wife at a time) or digamy (more than one legal wife in succession).

Three important observations can be made. First, although polygamy was known in the Jewish community of Paul's day, it was alien to the Graeco-Roman culture. Since Paul never mentioned polygamy in his extensive passages about marriage (and there is no evidence it was ever practiced by the early Christians), a warning against polygamous elders seems out of place. Second, whatever Paul was dealing with, it appears in the context of the elder's blamelessness. In Titus and in 1 Timothy the reading is that the elder must "be blameless, the husband of one wife" (Titus 1:6; 1 Tim. 3:2). Third, the work of the elder is associated with family life (1 Tim. 3:4-5), so that a close connection exists between a man's homelife and his suitability for a ministry over "the family of God." The office of the elder is so sensitive and so crucial that it requires a man of unassailable character and background. It would seem, therefore, that a divorced man would be prohibited from assuming this office, though not, of course, from countless other areas of service.

The eldership is also an office of leadership. Paul reminded Timothy that a man who could not rule his own house was not qualified to care for the church of God (1 Tim. 3:5). The word *rule* is from the Greek word *proistemi*, which means *to govern* or *to preside over with authority*. On the other hand, an elder who rules well (*proistemi*) is worthy of double honor (1 Tim. 5:17). There is no such thing as a strong church with a weak, ineffectual pastor. Nor is there ever a dynamic church that operates under the control of a small group of laymen. A *presbuteros*, an elder, a pastor, uniquely qualified by the calling of God, by the virtue and preparation of his life and by the closeness of his walk with the Savior, must lead his people as a shepherd. The church is rare that will disdain to follow and respect such a man.

The bishop. There could scarcely be a word more apt to summarize the ministry of a godly pastor than the Greek word *episkopos* (bishop). The noun comes from the verb *episkep-*

tomai, which means to look upon someone with regard or care. The word was used by the Greeks to describe the gracious care and oversight of their deities.

The use of the word by the early Christians, though, gives it a full-orbed splendor that sanctifies the labor of the ministry. In the New Testament, *episkeptomai* signifies a kind and degree of love and care that originated with God himself, and culminated in the gift of his only-begotten Son. Peter, for example, exhorted the elders to take the oversight (*episkopountes*) of the flock willingly (1 Pet. 5:2), reminding them that their example was Jesus Christ, "the Shepherd and Bishop [episkopon] of . . . [their] souls" (1 Pet. 2:25). When Stephen delivered his incomparable oration before the Sanhedrin, he declared that the lifelong burden of Moses for the children of Israel began when "it came into his heart to visit [*episkepsasthai*, literally bishop] his brethren" (Acts 7:23).

A bishop, an *episkopos,* is set apart for a labor that is unlike any other known to mankind. His life is committed to God's people. He lives among them. He rejoices with them in their triumphs and weeps with them in their tragedies. He endeavors to build them up in the Lord and lift them up when they fall. The spiritual life of his people is his continual burden and responsibility.

In this connection we understand Paul's instruction that a bishop must rule his own house well. The church that a man pastors is like his family. Notice how Timothy was told to treat the church people (1 Tim. 5:1-2). The pastor is to care for his church as though it were his own family.

In this connection we also understand the visitation ministry of a pastor. We often are inclined to think of the pastor's visitation as a kind of public relations program or as the congenial glue by which the factions of the church's social structure are held together. Scriptural visitation is neither. An example is Paul's concern for the churches he founded on his first missionary journey. After the Jerusalem Council he began to think about them and said to Barnabas, "Let us go again and visit our brethren in every city where we have preached the word of the Lord, and see how they do" (Acts 15:36). A public relations exercise? A social call? Emphatically not! The word *visit is episkepsometha*—"let us go . . . bishop . . . ." The pastor's visitation should have that kind of loving care, responsibility, and concern for edification. When it does, our churches, like those of Asia, will be established in the faith and will increase in number daily (Acts 16:5).

Unlike *presbuteros* and *poimen,* the word *episkopos* is never used anywhere in the New Testament as a title for an apostle, a prophet, or an evangelist. It is used only for the settled work of the pastor of a local church. The work of an *episkopos* is not work that can be done on a short term. It takes time. Short and flighty ministries can never build great, strong churches. If we believe Peter, the *episkopos* must enter a field with the same love, the same resolve with which our blessed Lord approached Calvary. He did not turn aside, whatever the agony, however costly the sacrifice, until the holy assignment had been consummated in an everlasting triumph.

PERSONAL LEARNING ACTIVITY 15
Write at least three paragraphs explaining how you have seen your pastor function as pastor, as elder, and as bishop. If you have difficulty distinguishing among the three functions, review the material you have just studied.

The Office of the Deacon
The origin. The Greek word *diakonos* has been taken into the English language as *deacon.* It is a common word, found in its different forms more than one hundred times in the New Testament. Of these one hundred occurrences, however, only five clearly refer to the deaconship of a local church.

The word *diakonos* was taken from the secular Greek world. Its basic meaning was "to wait at table, to serve as a table waiter." To the cultured Greek mind, such work was demeaning and unworthy. The ideal was to be served, never to serve.

In the New Testament the word retains the basic thought of "waiting at table," but it loses any suggestion of menial labor or subservience. To the contrary, it denotes the most noble work of man. The Savior claimed it for himself. He used this word when he said that he came "not to be ministered unto but to minister"—literally "to serve as a deacon."

This kind of ministry is for every Christian. In Ephesians 4:11-12, Paul declared that Christ gives various kinds of leaders to equip believers for "the work of the ministry" (*diakonias*). In the truest sense, we are all deacons, whether we pastor a church, preach as an evangelist, or labor as a layman. Why then an ordained body of deacons?

The New Testament does not say exactly how the deaconship got started. Most scholars agree, however, that Acts 6:1-6 either records the origin of the office of the deacon or at least foreshadows it.

As the early church grew, a dispute arose over the care of the widows (compare Acts 2:44-45; 4:34-35). The Greek-speaking Christians were disturbed because they thought the widows of their number were not being properly looked after. When the apostles heard of it, they said, "It is not reason that we should leave the word of God, and serve tables" (Acts 6:2). That phrase "and serve tables" comes from the Greek word *diakonein* (to deacon). The people were instructed to search out seven godly men who could be appointed "over this business" (Acts 6:3). Once chosen, they were set apart by prayer and the laying on of hands (Acts 6:6).

The requirements. Notice these three outstanding features of the record. First, these seven were elected to serve the men who preached the Word. Second, they were appointed to meet practical needs by whatever administrative means were required. The word *business* in Acts 6:3 is the Greek word *chreias,* which means literally *what will supply the need.* The emphasis is on meeting a need, not establishing a managerial board. Third, the seven were chosen on the basis of their walk with the Lord and their example (Acts 6:3). Each of these features is repeated in later instructions concerning the diaconate.

The deacon's relationship to the pastor is seen from Philippians 1:1 and 1 Timothy 3:1 and following, where we find the only uses of the word *deacon* as a title. In each instance, the word *deacon* is mentioned in relation with, and in subordination to, the pastor. It seems that the deacon's primary function is to serve the congregation on behalf of the pastor, freeing him for the vital task of ministering God's word to the people. Robert Naylor tells of a deacon he had in an early pastorate. Dr. Naylor asked the deacon to give up a class he loved and had built to take a struggling class of young boys. The deacon responded, "Whatever the pastor asks me to do, I'll do." The office of the deacon should be like that, a help to the pastor.

The deacon's task of meeting practical need can be seen in the word *diakonos*, table-server. Moreover, the qualifications of the deacon (1 Tim. 3:8-13) suggest such a work. For the most part, the qualifications for a deacon are the same as for a pastor (notice the words *in like manner*). There are, however, two notable exceptions. The deacon is to be *grave* and not *double-tongued* (1 Tim. 3:8). These requirements suggest a work among people with problems, where a loose tongue and a flippant or careless attitude could inflict great damage. And there is another suggestion in these qualifications that echoes Acts 6. The deacon's work of meeting needs has in view the harmony of the fellowship. Remember, the men of Acts 6 were chosen because of a murmuring.

Finally, it is plain that the deacons must be men of impeccable Christian character and example. They must be grounded firmly in the faith (1 Tim. 3:9), growing more firm as they fulfill the responsibilities of the office faithfully (1 Tim. 3:13). They must be men of proved character and ability (1 Tim. 3:10), exemplary domestic life (1 Tim. 3:12), and personal virtue (1 Tim. 3:8). Note also that Paul calls for a deacon, like a pastor, to be the husband of one wife.

Deaconesses. More and more frequently today, the question arises whether women should be permitted to serve as deacons, or as a separate group of deaconesses. The issue is raised primarily on three grounds. First, Paul commended a woman named Phoebe to the church at Rome as a "servant [*diakonon*] of the church which is at Cenchrea" (Rom. 16:1, NASB). Second, the reading of 1 Timothy 3:11 is unclear and could be translated, unlike the King James Version, "Even so must their [the deacons'] wives . . ."; but as in the Revised Standard Version, "The women likewise . . . ." Third, there is clear evidence that the early church recognized an office of deaconess as early as the third century.

Although there seems to be no support for the ordination of women as deacons, the question of deaconesses is more complex. The following factors, however, should be weighed. First, the word *diakonos* is rarely used as an official title. Although Phoebe is called a *diakonos*, so are many others who do not hold any official position. Second, strong arguments can be made that the women of 1 Timothy 3:11 are deaconesses or that they are wives of deacons who might be expected to participate in the delicate ministry of their husbands. Certainty about either interpretation is not possible. Third, the New Testament does not otherwise mention an office of deaconess.

On the positive side, however, there appears to have existed a quasi-official position of service for women in the first-century church. Such a position is suggested openly with regard to widows in 1 Timothy 5:3-6. Because the ministry of the deacons to unmarried women could give rise to difficult situations, it is possible that some godly women were set apart to help in that area. The Scriptures do not reveal how their ministry might have been handled. The records of the early post-apostolic church make plain, however, that the early church recognized such an office.

Whether or not a church interprets the Scriptures to allow for deaconesses, the ministry of godly women is essential if the needs of all believers are to be met. For the table-waiting ministry is a ministry for everyone.

FOR FURTHER STUDY

If you feel a need for further study in some of the areas dealt with in this chapter, you will find the following Equipping Center modules to be excellent for individual study or for group study.

Making Good Marriages Better
Deacons Training to Minister
Training Sunday School Workers in Outreach
Your Family: Learning, Loving, Living
Your Home and Christian Discipline

The Ordinance
of Baptism

Complete this short exercise before you begin studying the chapter on baptism. Doing so will help you organize your thoughts about baptism and will alert you to what you should learn from this chapter.

A. Cross out any inaccurate statements.
1. Baptism symbolizes Christ's death, burial, and resurrection.
2. Baptism symbolizes the believer's future resurrection.
3. Baptism is an act of obedience.
4. Baptism is God's means of expressing his approval of the believer.
5. Baptism should be administered only by a pastor.
6. Baptism is the believer's entrance into church membership.
7. Baptism is the believer's entrance into spiritual life.

B. The practice of infant baptism originated because—
1. the church wanted to express its watchcare over children
2. some believed unbaptized infants were lost
3. scholarship revealed that the New Testament church occasionally baptized children

C. The practice of sprinkling or pouring originated because—
1. it was more convenient to do so
2. the New Testament verb does not rule out this mode
3. this mode is not inconsistent with the symbolism of the ordinance

Chapter 6

The Ordinance
of Baptism

Christian baptism is the immersion of a believer in water in
the name of the Father, the Son, and the Holy Spirit. It is an
act of obedience symbolizing the believer's faith in a
crucified, buried, and risen Saviour, the believer's death to
sin, the burial of the old life, and the resurrection to walk in
newness of life in Christ Jesus. It is a testimony to his faith
in the final resurrection of the dead. Being a church ordinance, it is prerequisite to the privileges of church membership and to the Lord's Supper.

The Baptist Faith and Message (1963)

PERSONAL LEARNING ACTIVITY 16
**Did you complete the exercise on the facing page before
beginning this chapter? If you did not, take time to do so now.**

In a New Testament church there are only two ordinances—
baptism and the Lord's Supper. The ordinance of baptism was
given at the beginning of Christ's ministry, the ordinance of the
Lord's Supper at the close. Together they picture the most
crucial and important truths of the New Testament—the death,
burial, and resurrection of the Lord Jesus Christ. The Lord's
Supper symbolically depicts the broken body and shed blood of

our Lord; baptism visualizes his burial in the tomb of Joseph of Arimathea and his bodily resurrection on the third day. Foot washing is not considered an ordinance for two reasons: (1) historically, the apostles did not interpret the commandment of John 13:14 to mean that foot washing was to be considered a perpetual, symbolic ordinance of the church; (2) theologically, foot washing in no way serves as a picture of the atonement of the Lord Jesus Christ.

Some consider the doctrinal aspects of the ordinances to be unimportant. However, experience has shown that the church that is right on the ordinances will more than likely be right on the other great doctrines of the faith (and vice versa).

Baptists consistently have used the word *ordinance* rather than *sacrament,* because the latter term conveys the idea that baptism and the Lord's Supper have saving power. Such a notion, however, is completely foreign to the New Testament. The English word *ordinance* is derived from the Latin *ordinare,* which means *to set in order* in the sense of something being authoritatively ordained or decreed. The term has been applied specifically to baptism and the Lord's Supper to indicate that they are sacred and symbolic acts divinely instituted and commanded by the Lord (Matt. 28:19-20; 1 Cor. 11:24).

THE BEGINNING OF BAPTISM

The Baptism of John

The Bible makes two important claims about the baptism of John. First, the baptism of John was indeed from heaven (Matt. 21:25; Mark 11:30-31). Second, the commission and pattern for baptism were given to John by God (John 1:33) and were accepted by Jesus (Matt. 3:15).

Although the baptism of John might have had its roots in the Jewish practice of proselyte baptism (the initiatory rite for Gentile converts into Judaism), the two were not identical. Proselyte baptism was probably semiprivate; John's baptism was public. Proselyte baptism was doubtlessly self-administered; in John's baptism there was an administrator. Proselyte baptism signified a change in creed (from paganism to Judaism); John's baptism signified and presupposed a change of heart. Proselyte baptism was for Gentiles only; John's baptism was for Jews as well.

The Baptism of Jesus

The Scriptures expressly state that John baptized Jesus (Matt. 3:13-17; Mark 1:9-11; Luke 3:21-23). The Scriptures also give abundant testimony to the fact that Christ was sinless (2 Cor. 5:21; Heb. 4:15; 7:26; 1 Pet. 2:22; 1 John 3:5). Why, then, did Jesus submit to a baptism based on repentance? There are three reasons. (1) Jesus was identifying his ministry with that of John the Baptist. (2) Jesus was setting an example for his disciples of all generations to follow. (3) Jesus publicly was dedicating himself to his redemptive ministry. The baptism of Jesus served as a transition from the baptism of John to the baptism practiced by the New Testament church.

THE NEW TESTAMENT CONCEPT OF BAPTISM

The New Testament doctrine of baptism is considered under five main headings: (1) the meaning of baptism, (2) the candidate for baptism, (3) the mode of baptism, (4) the authority for baptism, and (5) the purpose of baptism.

The Meaning of Baptism

The Scriptures clearly state that baptism was given to John the Baptist from heaven (Matt. 21:25). What did God have in mind in establishing such an initiatory rite? Baptism gives the church and the world a past, present, and future testimony. Baptism points to the death, burial, and resurrection of Christ (past). Baptism illustrates how the believer dies to sin and is raised to a new life in Christ (present). Water baptism is also a prophetic testimony to the future bodily resurrection of all believers (future). The classic passage on the meaning of baptism is Romans 6:3-11.

Baptism symbolizes the death, burial, and resurrection of Christ. Baptism visualizes Christ's death on the cross, his burial which followed, and his resurrection from the dead on the third day (Rom. 6:3-4). The most concise description of the gospel is 1 Corinthians 15:3-4: "I delivered unto you first of all that which I also received, how that Christ died for our sins according to the scriptures; and that he was buried, and that he rose again the third day according to the scriptures." When a person enters the waters of baptism, is immersed, and is raised up, he points to that event in history when Jesus Christ—fully God and fully man—died on the cross, was buried in the tomb of Joseph of Arimathea, and was raised again on the third day. In water baptism the believer affirms his faith in the most crucial truths of the New Testament. God's great redemptive act of the Old Testament—the Exodus—was viewed by Paul as a type of baptism (1 Cor. 10:2). God's great redemptive act of the New Testament—the death, burial, and resurrection of Christ—is reenacted in the water baptism of every believer.

Baptism symbolizes the present death and resurrection of believers. First, you should understand clearly that baptism is not administered for the remission of sin. The blood of Jesus Christ and his blood alone cleanses from sin (Eph. 1:7; 1 John 1:7). Water baptism does not effect salvation. It assumes that salvation has taken place and symbolizes it.

Water baptism pictures the identification of the believer with Christ in a spiritual death, burial, and resurrection—"Therefore we are buried with him by baptism into death: that like as Christ was raised up from the dead by the glory of the Father, even so we also should walk in newness of life" (Rom. 6:4). Through baptism the believer shows that he has died to sin, that his old life has been buried with Christ, and that he has been raised up to walk in newness of life with Christ. Only the dead are buried; only those who have died to sin can arise to newness of life. Thus, in the ordinance of baptism, the believer declares his intent to live a holy and sanctified life. Baptism is a public testimony that one had abandoned his old way of life for a new way of life. "How shall we, that are dead to sin, live any longer therein?" (Rom. 6:2).

Baptism symbolizes the future bodily resurrection of all believers. The ordinance of baptism is also closely related to last things. This prophetic aspect of baptism is seen in the fact that it is a visual testimony to the future bodily resurrection of all believers, "If we have been planted together in the likeness of his death, we shall be also in the likeness of his resurrection" (Rom. 6:5). Baptism depicts a marvelous hope and promise. One of the central doctrines of the Christian faith is the belief in the bodily resurrection of all believers who die before the return

Doug Brachey

Baptism symbolizes three fundamental truths of the Christian faith—one related to the past, one to the present, and one to the future.

of our blessed Lord (1 Cor. 15:52). Baptism, then, is an expression of faith in one's own future bodily resurrection.

The Candidate for Baptism

One of the greatest problems the church faces today is that of unconverted church members. The doctrine that a rebirth experience is a necessary prerequisite to baptism and church membership cannot be emphasized too strongly.

A confession of faith in Christ was an integral part of New Testament baptism (Acts 2:41; 8:37-38; 10:43-48). Baptists have insisted on believer's baptism—the baptism of those who make a personal confession of faith in Jesus Christ as Lord. We believe the order of the Great Commission to be just as inspired as the content. That order is conversion, baptism, church membership (Matt. 28:19-20; Acts 2:41-42). The command to baptize is conditioned on one's first becoming a disciple. Proclaiming the gospel must always precede baptism, for "faith cometh by hearing, and hearing by the word of God" (Rom. 10:17). It is through the faithfully declaring the gospel, and not baptism, that disciples are made (Acts 2:41-42; Rom. 10:17; 1 Cor. 1:21).

In the New Testament, baptism is administered to believers only. There is no instance where someone who had not already been converted was baptized. Some theologians argue that there must have been some babies in the Philippian jailor's household, but a close study of the text reveals that every member of his family believed in God (Acts 16:34), indicating that even the younger members were old enough to make a personal commitment of their lives to the Lord Jesus Christ. The example of Cornelius and his household further substantiates this fact. It is quite evident from Acts 10:47 ("Can any man forbid water, that these should not be baptized, which have received the Holy Ghost as well as we?") that conversion is to precede baptism, and that one is not ready for baptism until regeneration has taken place.

Unfortunately, millions of people share a superstitious belief that if a baby dies before he is sprinkled, the baby is lost and goes to hell. However, innumerable multitudes believe that if a child dies before he reaches the age of accountability, he goes immediately to be with the Lord, whether he has been sprinkled or not (2 Sam. 12:22-23; Matt. 18:1-10). In the marvelous grace of God, provision is made for the atonement of the child's sins.

Infant baptism is rejected as nonscriptural for two reasons. First, there is no example of infant baptism in the New Testament. Proponents of infant baptism erroneously assume that Christ's blessing the children (Matt. 19:13-15; Mark 10:13-16; Luke 18:15-17) included baptism. However, there is no indication in the entire passage that baptism took place. In the household baptisms of Acts (Cornelius, 10:24-48; Lydia, 16:15; Philippian jailor, 16:31-34; and Crispus, 18:8), there is not the slightest indication that infants were baptized. To suggest that the apostolic church practiced infant baptism is a hazardous and precarious inference. Second, there is no stated precept for infant baptism in the New Testament. To the contrary, Christ commanded his disciples first to make disciples and then to baptize them. Infant baptism cannot meet this criterion.

Although infant baptism did not come into prominence until the fifth century, a sacramental view of baptism began to develop as early as the second century. Justin Martyr (c. AD 100-165) used John 3:3,5 to teach that baptism was an instrumental means of salvation. Thus, in actuality, the practice of infant baptism stemmed from the erroneous notion of baptismal regeneration.

Although there is some evidence for infant baptism as early as the second century, it was the theology of Augustine (AD 354-430) that fully defended the practice. As the doctrines of original sin and baptismal regeneration came to dominate the theology of the church, infant baptism became the rule rather than the exception. With the development of infant baptism, there was a change from immersion to sprinkling to accommodate the practice of baptizing infants. From the fifth century onward, infant baptism was customarily administered prior to the eighth day after birth, thus making infant baptism a New Testament counterpart to Old Testament circumcision. Baptism upon profession of faith is the only effective safeguard against the dangerous misconceptions of baptismal regeneration and infant baptism.

Those who are baptized are to be believers. Baptism, even by immersion, is not valid if the person being baptized is not already saved. What should a person who is already a member of a Baptist church do when he realizes that his baptism came before his salvation? The answer is obvious. He should be baptized. This is not, as some would object, being baptized again, for his first immersion was not really baptism. Only when a person is a believer is immersion genuinely New Testament baptism.

Baptizing for the dead appears to be a growing practice today among some cults, particularly Mormons. In the one mysterious reference to the practice in the New Testament (1 Cor. 15:29), Paul was not supporting baptism for those who had already died; he was making reference to the practice for the sake of substantiating his argument for the bodily resurrection. In no way can the passage be construed to mean that Paul advocated that believers be baptized for those who had already died to secure their salvation.

The Mode of Baptism

The following facts give evidence that immersion is the only mode of scriptural baptism: (1) the basic meaning of *baptizo*, from which we get our English word *baptism*, is *to immerse*; (2) the actual baptism accounts in the New Testament picture immersion as the mode; (3) the meaning of baptism—death, burial, and resurrection—is lost in any mode other than immersion; (4) the practice of the early church indicates that immersion was the correct mode of baptism. Each tenet is worthy of examination.

The meaning of baptizo. The word translated *baptize* in the New Testament (*baptizo*, Greek) means *to dip, to plunge, to submerge, to immerse.* No competent Greek scholar would suggest otherwise. A tour group in the Holy Land and the cities of Paul asked a tour guide in Athens, "What does the word *baptizo* mean in Greek today?" His reply was, "It means to immerse, to get inside the water." The word has always meant just that; it has never been used to denote sprinkling or pouring. The Greek language of the New Testament has words for *sprinkle* and *pour,* but these words are never used to refer to baptism.

New Testament baptismal accounts. Immersion was clearly

the practice of the early church. The New Testament accounts of baptism certainly lead to the conclusion that immersion is the only scriptural mode of baptism. Jesus was baptized in (*eis*, Greek) the Jordan River, not on the banks (Mark 1:9). After he was immersed, he came up out of (*ek*, Greek) the water. In the account of the baptism of the Ethiopian eunuch, the Scriptures state that "they both went down into [*eis*, Greek] the water" (Acts 8:38, NASB), and "they came up out of [*ek*, Greek] the water" (Acts 8:39, NASB).

The meaning of baptism. If baptism is a symbol of the believer's identification with the death, burial, and resurrection of the Lord Jesus (Rom. 6:3-11), the mode must correspond accurately to the symbol. In fact, the mode either verifies or nullifies the meaning of the symbol. Pouring or sprinkling does not symbolize what baptism should portray. Immersion is the only mode that accurately depicts the biblical meaning of baptism. All other modes lose their theological significance and degenerate into meaningless initiation rites.

The practice of the early church. The New Testament church immersed new converts. No competent New Testament scholar would deny that immersion was the mode of baptism of the apostolic church. Why, then, did immersion not remain the mode of baptism?

Probably the earliest reference to baptism outside the New Testament is to be found in the *Didache*, a second-century work known also as *The Teaching of the Twelve Apostles*. This work contains the first known diversion from immersion, allowing for affusion or pouring in cases where sufficient water was not available. As the doctrine of baptismal regeneration gained prominence in the church, the practices of clinical baptism (pouring water over a sick or invalid person) and infant baptism (sprinkling water over an infant) became the accepted practices of the day.

When the Catholic Church divided into the Roman and Greek branches in AD 1054, the Greek branch retained immersion as its mode of baptism. Sprinkling did not become the official mode of baptism for the Roman Catholic Church until the thirteenth century. In Europe, Catholic churches built before the thirteenth century often display murals or mosaics showing the baptism of Jesus by immersion rather than by sprinkling. In the Roman cathedral in Pisa, Italy, completed in the twelfth century, there is a spacious and beautiful baptistry!

During the Reformation the major emphasis was on believer's baptism rather than on the mode, the issue being believer's baptism as opposed to infant baptism. By the time of the Reformation, immersion generally had been abandoned by all groups except the Greek Orthodox Church. By the middle of the seventeenth century, however, the mode became a crucial issue among Baptists. The First London Confession of 1644 spelled out two significant things about baptism: (1) that baptism be administered only to those professing faith in Christ, that is, believer's baptism as against infant baptism; (2) that immersion—dipping or plunging the whole body under water—be the only manner of administering baptism. These two crucial doctrinal tenets were restated in the Second London Confession of 1677, one of the most important of all Baptist confessions.

In the United States, both the Philadelphia Confession (1742) and the New Hampshire Confession (1833) stressed believer's baptism by immersion only. The New Hampshire Confession served as the basis for the first "Baptist Faith and Message" (1925), a statement of faith generally adopted by local churches of the Southern Baptist Convention. "The Baptist Faith and Message" adopted by the Southern Baptist Convention in 1963 states again the dual Baptist distinctives of baptism of believers only and by immersion only.

The Authority for Baptism

In the New Testament, responsibility for performing the ordinances is not specifically assigned to the church. However, it is logical and natural to assume that this is the church's responsibility. The authority for baptism, by precept (Matt. 28:19) and by example (Matt. 3:13), rests with Christ himself. As Christ is viewed as the Head of the church (Eph. 1:22), the authority for the administration of the ordinances rests with the local church. Baptists generally, and Southern Baptists in particular, have consistently held that baptism and the Lord's Supper are church ordinances, that is, they are to be viewed as congregational rather than as individual acts. Both baptism and the Lord's Supper are a part of the church's public witness and testimony.

The authority to baptize has to lie somewhere. Someone has to receive or reject the candidate. Southern Baptists believe the local church is the logical biblical authority. Administering the ordinances apart from the local church results in confusion. Thus, baptism is to be administered only by a person authorized by the local church to do so. Usually, that person is the pastor, but this need not always be the case. The local church may authorize whomever it wishes to administer baptism. In Acts 10, Peter turned to the brethren and called for a vote about the new converts in Caesarea: "Can any man forbid water, that these should not be baptized, which have received the Holy Ghost as well as we?" (Acts 10:47). That is what I do when a man comes forward having accepted Jesus as his personal Savior. I ask the people if they are ready to receive him as a candidate for baptism into the fellowship of our church. But it is the church that authorizes the convert's baptism. The Scriptures are silent about the authority for the baptism of the Ethiopian eunuch (Acts 8). Did the church at Jerusalem authorize Philip to baptize? We do not know.

The ordinances, however, are not invested in a man, not even the pastor of the church. A pastor might one day prove to be a reprobate—a thief, a liar, or even a murderer; but this would not nullify the validity of baptisms he had administered. The validity of baptism simply is not dependent on the integrity or piety of the administrator.

Baptist churches today are faced with the problem of what to do about alien immersion—receiving those who have been immersed in other faiths. The reason Southern Baptists have rejected baptism by sprinkling or pouring is obvious—it is not New Testament baptism. But why do most Southern Baptist churches reject the baptism of those who practice immersion for salvation? The same principle applies. Even though a group may use the proper mode, if the meaning is sacramental rather than symbolic, it is not New Testament baptism. Neither the mode nor the meaning can be changed. Biblical baptism requires the proper meaning as well as the correct mode.

The Purpose of Baptism

Although Baptists reject baptismal regeneration, we must guard against minimizing the importance of baptism. Not only is it important that men be saved before baptism; it is also vital that men be baptized after they are saved. Christ did not suggest baptism; he commanded it (Matt. 28:19). Why, then, is baptism so important? The ordinance of baptism actually serves three purposes.

First, baptism is a public testimony. Being baptized is a convert's open declaration of his faith in the literal death, burial, and resurrection of the Lord Jesus Christ. The believer testifies by his baptism that he has experienced in his own life the saving power of Christ's death, burial, and resurrection. As baptism is a public declaration of faith in Christ, it should follow soon after one's conversion experience. In the New Testament, when a person received Christ, the church gave testimony to that fact by baptizing him immediately (Acts 2:41; 9:18; 10:47-48; 16:15,33).

Second, baptism is an act of loving obedience to the explicit command of the Lord (Matt. 28:19-20). Although baptism is not essential to salvation, it is essential to obedience. "If ye love me, keep my commandments" (John 14:15).

Third, the believer identifies himself with Christ and the local fellowship of believers through baptism. In water baptism the new believer identifies himself with the Head of the church, the Lord Jesus Christ, and also with the body of the Lord, the local church.

PERSONAL LEARNING ACTIVITY 17

Review the way you completed the exercise at the beginning of this chapter. You should have no difficulty determining the correctness of your responses. Make any changes that are necessary.

PERSONAL LEARNING ACTIVITY 18
Think back to the occasion of your baptism. Try to recall the understanding you had at that time about the experience you were having. List truths about baptism you did not have at the time but came to know later. Then list the misunderstanding you had about baptism at that time but came to understand later.

CONCLUSION

There is ample evidence that Christ intended his followers to practice baptism. (1) Christ himself was baptized, thus setting an example for us to follow (Matt. 3:13-17). (2) He commanded his disciples to baptize their converts (Matt. 28:19-20). (3) The apostles both taught and practiced baptism in the New Testament church (Acts 2:38,41; 8:12-13,36-38; 9:18; 10:47-48; 16:15-33). To be a genuine New Testament church in faith and practice demands that a local church baptize its converts.

1 CORINTHIANS 11:18-29

I am told that when you meet as a congregation you fall into sharply divided groups; and I believe there is some truth in it (for dissensions are necessary if only to show which of your members are sound). The result is that when you meet as a congregation, it is impossible for you to eat the Lord's Supper, because each of you is in such a hurry to eat his own, and while one goes hungry another has too much to drink. Have you no homes of your own to eat and drink in? Or are you so contemptuous of the church of God that you shame its poorer members? What am I to say? Can I commend you? On this point, certainly not!

For the tradition which I handed on to you came to me from the Lord himself: that the Lord Jesus, on the night of his arrest, took bread and, after giving thanks to God, broke it and said: "This is my body, which is for you; do this as a memorial of me." In the same way, he took the cup after supper, and said: "This cup is the new covenant sealed by my blood. Whenever you drink it, do this as a memorial of me." For every time you eat this bread and drink the cup, you proclaim the death of the Lord, until he comes.

It follows that anyone who eats the bread or drinks the cup of the Lord unworthily will be guilty of desecrating the body and blood of the Lord. A man must test himself before eating his share of the bread and drinking from the cup. For he who eats and drinks eats and drinks judgement on himself if he does not discern the Body.

NEB

18 For first of all, when ye come together in the church, I hear that there be divisions among you; and I partly believe it.

19 For there must be also heresies among you, that they which are approved may be made manifest among you.

20 When ye come together therefore into one place, *this* is not to eat the Lord's supper.

21 For in eating every one taketh before *other* his own supper: and one is hungry, and another is drunken.

22 What? have ye not houses to eat and to drink in? or despise ye the church of God, and shame them that have not? What shall I say to you? shall I praise you in this? I praise *you* not.

23 For I have received of the Lord that which also I delivered unto you, That the Lord Jesus the *same* night in which he was betrayed took bread:

24 And when he had given thanks, he brake *it*, and said, Take, eat: this is my body, which is broken for you: this do in remembrance of me.

25 After the same manner also *he* took the cup, when he had supped, saying, This cup is the new testament in my blood: this do ye, as oft as ye drink *it*, in remembrance of me.

26 For as often as ye eat this bread, and drink this cup, ye do shew the Lord's death till he come.

27 Wherefore whosoever shall eat this bread, and drink *this* cup of the Lord, unworthily, shall be guilty of the body and blood of the Lord.

28 But let a man examine himself, and so let him eat of *that* bread, and drink of *that* cup.

29 For he that eateth and drinketh unworthily, eateth and drinketh damnation to himself, not discerning the Lord's body.

KJV

Chapter 7

The Ordinance of the Lord's Supper

The Lord's Supper is a symbolic act of obedience whereby members of the church, through partaking of the bread and the fruit of the vine, memorialize the death of the Redeemer and anticipate His second coming.

The Baptist Faith and Message (1963)

The other ordinance of the church is the Lord's Supper. Baptism by immersion is a once-for-all act of obedience that should follow one's conversion immediately. The Lord's Supper, in contrast, is to be observed periodically and perpetually by all believers until the return of the Lord. This chapter examines the Lord's Supper from four perspectives: (1) the institution of the Lord's Supper, (2) erroneous theories of the Lord's Supper, (3) the meaning of the Lord's Supper, and (4) practical considerations about the Lord's Supper.

THE INSTITUTION OF THE LORD'S SUPPER

The Passover of the Old Testament

The Gospels are specific in pointing out that the Lord's Supper was instituted within the context of the Jewish Passover, the most important of the Old Testament feasts (Matt. 26:17; Mark 14:12; Luke 22:7). Perhaps one reason that the Lord's Supper apparently does not mean as much to the twentieth-century church as it did to the first-century church is that Christians really do not understand the Old Testament background.

The great redemptive act of the Old Testament was the Exodus—God's deliverance of the children of Israel out of the bondage of Egyptian slavery (Ex. 12). To commemorate this, God instituted the Passover, to be observed on the evening of the fourteenth day of the first month of the Jewish year (Ex. 12:2-3). This is in late March or early April. The feast was meant to be an annual testimony to God's deliverance of the children of Israel out of the bondage of Egypt. Each year the Israelites were to retell the story of God's redemption and reenact the first feast. This kept God's deliverance fresh in their minds and instructed their children in what God had done in their behalf. What the Passover was to the Old Testament, the Lord's Supper is to the New Testament.

The Last Supper

On the eve of the crucifixion, the Lord gathered with his disciples to observe the Passover meal. Jesus did not eat the Passover a day early, as some erroneously conclude (Matt. 26:17; Mark 14:12; Luke 22:7). The Passover was on Thursday night; and the Gospel writers say unanimously that Jesus was crucified on preparation day (Friday), the day of preparation for the Jewish sabbath (Matt. 27:62; Mark 15:42; Luke 23:54; John 19:31). The crucifixion's occurrence at Passover time and Jesus' institution of the Lord's Supper at the Passover meal inseparably connect the two events and the two meals. The Passover was instituted the night before God provided deliverance from the bondage of slavery; the Lord's Supper was instituted the night before God provided deliverance from the bondage of sin.

ERRONEOUS THEORIES OF THE LORD'S SUPPER

Transubstantiation

The Roman Catholic theory of the Lord's Supper is known as *transubstantiation*. According to this view, when the priest consecrates the bread and the wine, the two are transformed into the actual body and actual blood of Christ. In other words, the elements of the Supper are literally transformed in substance, so that the participant is said to eat the body and drink

Nancy Robinson

The Lord's Supper is a symbolic act of obedience whereby the members of the church memorialize the death of the Redeemer and anticipate his second coming.

the blood of Jesus.

When Jesus said, "This is my body" (Matt. 26:26; Mark 14:22; Luke 22:19; 1 Cor. 11:24), it is obvious that he was speaking symbolically, unless there were two bodies of Christ present at that time. Not only does such a view savor of cannibalism, it denies the finality and completeness of the sacrifice of Christ on the cross (Heb. 9:28). Also, the laity are given only the bread, and the priesthood alone receive both elements.

Consubstantiation

The similar but somewhat modified view advocated by Martin Luther and adopted by the Lutheran Church is known as *consubstantiation*. Luther rejected the Roman Catholic view that the elements of the Supper actually are transformed into the body and blood of the Lord. Instead, he advocated the theory that the invisible and mystical presence of Christ is present "in, with, and under" the elements when a believer partakes of the Supper. The real presence of Christ, then, comes into the believer through the blood and wine of the Supper. This interpretation is just as wrong as the previous one, for both theories result in a magical kind of Christianity whereby a person is saved by taking communion instead of by believing on the Lord Jesus Christ.

The Reformed View

This theory is not quite as clear and as definite as the previous two and hence is more difficult to grasp. Denying both the Catholic and Luthern theories, while at the same time affirming that the elements used in the Supper are more than symbolic, this view affirms that Christ is present in the elements in a dynamic or spiritual sense. This position, however, still holds that the Lord's Supper is a sacrament, as do the first two, in that the observance of the Supper is a means of conferring grace to the communicant.

THE MEANING OF THE LORD'S SUPPER

Baptists have held to the belief that the Lord's Supper is symbolic in its significance. This is not to deny the spiritual omnipresence of Christ, but it is to deny that the elements of the

Supper convey and mediate the presence of Christ in a sacramental or grace-bearing manner. A denial of these three views necessitates a careful examination of the symbolic view, the view Baptists hold to be the scriptural position.

The most informative and instructive passage in the New Testament on the meaning of the Lord's Supper is 1 Corinthians 11:23-34. In the passage, Paul brought out some significant doctrinal truths; he taught that the Lord's Supper is (1) a memorial meal, (2) a thanksgiving meal, (3) a fellowship meal, (4) a covenant meal, (5) a testimonial meal, (6) a prophetic meal, and (7) an examination meal.

PERSONAL LEARNING ACTIVITY 19
Before studying further in this text, study the Scripture passage at the beginning of this chapter. Identify and underline words and phrases that indicate that the Lord's Supper is a memorial meal, a thanksgiving meal, a fellowship meal, a covenant meal, a testimonial meal, a prophetic meal, and an examination meal. As you study the following section, check your work.

The Lord's Supper as a Memorial Meal
In regard to the Supper, Jesus said, "This do in remembrance of me" (1 Cor. 11:24). When believers observe the Lord's Supper, they are to remember that Jesus gave himself as a sacrifice for sin. Note the preposition *for* in 1 Corinthians 11:24: "This is my body, which is broken *for* you." That preposition *for* (*huper*, Greek) means *in behalf of*. It means that Jesus has done something in our behalf that we could never do for ourselves. Only Jesus on the cross could have secured redemption for sin.

The Lord's Supper is a perpetual reminder that it was the death of Jesus that secured atonement for sin. When the believer comes to the Lord's table, he is to remember that Jesus died for him. As the Passover served as a remembrance of God's deliverance of the Israelites from the bondage of Egyptian slavery, the Lord's Supper, for the Christian, serves as a perpetual reminder of Christ's deliverance of unbelievers from sin.

Some years ago, one of our Southern Baptist magazines carried a story about a boy named Tim. Tim was a Junior-age boy who had a younger sister with a serious disease. In fact, the doctors did not know if she would live. One day, after talking to the father, explaining the situation, and obtaining his permission, the doctor brought young Tim into his office and said: "Tim, you know how sick your little sister is. You are the only person we know who has the right kind of blood for her. Would you be willing to give your blood so that your sister might live?" Tim straightened up in his chair and his little chin began to tremble; it was almost as if he couldn't speak. Then the words came out, "Doctor, if giving my blood will make my little sister live, I'll do it." Because of the urgency of the hour, arrangements were made immediately. Tim and his sister were wheeled into the proper hospital room for the blood transfusion. Then, in a little while, after the transfusion was over, Tim raised up, looked at the doctor, and said, "Doctor, now when will I die?" Tim had been under the impression that if he gave his blood to his little sister, it would mean that he himself would die. But he was still willing to give his blood that his sister might live. That's just the way it was with out Lord. He was willing to give his blood on the cross that we might live. When you come to the Lord's table, you are to remember that Jesus died for you.

The Lord's Supper as a Thanksgiving Meal
When the Lord instituted the Supper with the apostles, he offered a prayer of thanks: "When he had given thanks, . . ." (1 Cor. 11:24; see also Matt. 26:26-27; Mark 14:22-23; Luke 22:19-22). The word translated *had given thanks* is the Greek word *eucharisteo,* which means *to be thankful, to give thanks.* Although *eucharist* is a good New Testament word, Baptists usually have felt uncomfortable with its use because of its association with sacramental theology. Nevertheless, it stresses the thanksgiving nature of the Lord's Supper.

The Lord's Supper is to be a joyous time for the people of

God, because they are celebrating the fact that God has redeemed them from their sins. Believers are to praise the name of the Lord who has redeemed them through his precious blood. The observance of the Lord's Supper should be a time when believers give thanks for what the Lord has done in their behalf.

The Lord's Supper as a Fellowship Meal

In his instructions to the Corinthian church about the Lord's Supper, Paul expressed concern for the divisiveness in the church. Note 1 Corinthians 11:18: "First of all, when ye come together in the church, I hear that there be divisions among you." Paul's judgment was that the church really could not observe the Lord's Supper until the spirit of fellowship had been restored (1 Cor. 11:20). It would revolutionize our churches if we could restore the fellowship aspect of the Lord's Supper. When a church came to the Lord's table and there existed a spirit of ill will among some of the members, suppose the pastor would say: "There is a spirit of divisiveness in the church. We cannot observe the Lord's Supper. To do so is hypocrisy. Let us pray together. We must be right with one another before we sit together at the Lord's table." Imagine what would happen in our churches if the Lord's Supper were always a genuine fellowship meal.

In 1 Corinthians 10:16, the Greek word translated *communion* is *koinonia*, which means fellowship. Paul's use of the word stresses the Supper as a *communion* (*koinonia*, Greek). This word stresses the sharing or fellowship aspect of the Lord's Supper. In any true observance of the Supper, believers should experience fellowship (communion) with Christ and with one another. In the next verse (1 Cor. 10:17), Paul argued that there should be unity in the church because they all partook of one loaf in the observance of the Supper. The Lord's Supper served as a visible demonstration of the fellowship of the body of Christ as all members partook of one loaf and one cup. The use of "many crumbs and many cups" is more sanitary, but the significant symbolism pictured by the one loaf and one cup is lost in our modern practice.

The Lord's Supper as a Covenant Meal

It is quite evident that Jesus looked on the juice of the Lord's Supper as being symbolic of the new covenant: "This cup is the new testament (literally *covenant; diatheke,* Greek) in my blood . . ." (1 Cor. 11:25; see also Matt. 26:28; Mark 14:24; Luke 22:20; Heb. 9:16-22). The literal meaning of the Greek word translated *testament* is *covenant.* The juice represents the blood of the new covenant. It is equivalent to covenant blood. The Mosaic covenant was ratified with blood (Ex. 24). When the burnt offerings and the peace offerings were slain, half of the blood was sprinkled upon the altar. Moses flung the other half upon the people and exclaimed, "Behold the blood of the covenant" (Ex. 24:8). Likewise, the new covenant also was inaugurated with blood, the precious blood of the Lord Jesus Christ. The new covenant of redemption is an unbreakable blood covenant, vouchsafed by the blood of Christ himself (Heb. 8:6-13). It is the blood of the Lord Jesus that guarantees the believer's salvation for all eternity. The Lord's Supper serves as a perpetual reminder of that guarantee.

The Lord's Supper as a Testimonial Meal

In 1 Corinthians 11:26 Paul said an amazing thing about the Lord's Supper: "Ye do *shew* the Lord's death till he come." That word translated *shew* is one of the New Testament words for *preach.* It means to *proclaim, to declare, to tell thoroughly, to preach.* In the King James Bible, ten of the occurrences are translated with the English word *preach* (Acts 4:2; 13:5,38; 15:36; 17:3, 13; 1 Cor. 9:14; Phil. 1:16,18; Col. 1:28). When the local church comes together to observe the Lord's Supper, it literally is preaching a sermon on the Lord's death and his return. Each time you observe the Lord's Supper, you preach the atoning death of our Lord and his future return. You proclaim it; declare it; you act it out as a testimony to all who are present.

The Lord's Supper as a Prophetic Meal

Look at the prophetic phrase "till he come" (1 Cor. 11:26). The Scriptures clearly teach the second coming of our Lord: "The Lord himself shall descend from heaven with a shout, with the voice of the archangel, and with the trump of God: and the dead in Christ shall rise first: then we which are alive and remain shall be caught up together with them in the clouds, to meet the Lord in the air: and so shall we ever be with the Lord" (1 Thess. 4:16-17). When the Lord returns for his people, he will have a reserved seat for every believer at a great heavenly banquet. The Bible calls it the "marriage supper of the Lamb" (Rev. 19:9). While the church remains on the earth, she is to continue to observe the Lord's Supper; however, the day will come when the Lord's Supper will be superseded by the marriage supper of the Lamb. Presently, the church observes the Lord's Supper in anticipation of his coming; however, the observation of the marriage supper will be in celebration of his coming. The Lord's Supper is an earnest of what it will be like when believers sit down at the marriage supper of the Lamb.

The Lord's Supper as an Examination Meal

The Lord's Supper should serve also as a time of both personal and congregational examination. Look at what Paul said in 1 Corinthians 11:27-29: "Wherefore whosoever shall eat this bread, and drink this cup of the Lord, unworthily, shall be guilty of the body and blood of the Lord. But let a man examine himself, and so let him eat of that bread, and drink of that cup. For he that eateth and drinketh unworthily, eateth and drinketh damnation to himself, not discerning the Lord's body." The passage is a warning of impending judgment to anyone who would come to the Lord's table for any reason other than to memorialize the atoning death of the Lord Jesus Christ. To come to the Lord's table while at odds with your brothers and sisters in the church before seeking reconciliation is to partake of the Lord's Supper in an unworthy manner.

The injunction, however, is often misunderstood. I have known many godly and well-meaning Christians who would not take the Lord's Supper, saying in their hearts, I am not worthy to take the Lord's Supper. But the Greek word translated *unworthily* is an adverb, not an adjective. Paul was not saying that a person must be worthy to take the Lord's Supper. He was saying that the manner in which it is done must not be unworthy. If it were a matter of being worthy to sit at the Lord's table, we would all be excluded. Based on our own personal righteousness, we are as men clothed in filthy rags (Isa. 64:6). But having been justified by his blood (Rom. 5:9) through personal faith (Rom. 5:1), we stand in the righteousness of Jesus Christ and not on our own merit. Therefore, each of us who is a believer is worthy, in Christ, to come to the Lord's table.

Nevertheless, the believer ought to examine himself carefully every time he comes to the Lord's table. As he partakes of the Lord's Supper, he ought to allow the Holy Spirit to search his heart and soul and to ask the Lord to cleanse and take away everything unacceptable to him. If such a period of examination takes place, the Lord's Supper will be a time of rededication and reconsecration within the church.

PERSONAL LEARNING ACTIVITY 20
Eucharist and *communion* are words Baptists seldom use to refer to the Lord's Supper. Explain why these should be considered perfectly acceptable words as long as they are used in the biblical sense.

PRACTICAL CONSIDERATIONS
ABOUT THE LORD'S SUPPER

Who Should Participate in the Supper?
Obviously, there is no place for unbelievers at the Lord's table. One who does not know the Lord cannot remember the Lord. Further, it has been the general position of Southern Baptists that only those who have been scripturally baptized should partake of the Lord's Supper.

The ordinance of baptism logically precedes that of the Lord's Supper. This is a reasonable deduction for several reasons. First, the practice of the New Testament church, in which baptism promptly followed conversion, meant that those who came to the Lord's table were already baptized. There is not a single example of a believer observing the Lord's Supper prior to baptism, while there are several illustrations of believers partaking of the Lord's Supper after baptism (Acts 2:41-42; 1 Cor. 11:20). Second, the symbolism of the ordinances necessitates this order. Union with Christ (baptism) naturally precedes communion with Christ (Lord's Supper). The two ordinances logically belong in that order. Third, this order is given in the Great Commission (Matt. 28:19-20), which states: (1) to make disciples, (2) to baptize them, and (3) to teach them to observe all things that Christ commanded, which, of course, would naturally include the Lord's Supper. Fourth, the analogy of the Old Testament Passover serves to confirm this order. In the Old Testament, circumcision served as the sign of the old covenant, and Exodus 12:48 specifically states that in ancient Israel a man was to bear in his body the sign of the covenant (circumcision) before he ate of the Passover meal. The sign of the new covenant is water baptism. When a person becomes a Christian, he is to be baptized. It has been the overwhelming view of Southern Baptists that one who comes to the Lord's table ought to have in his body the sign of the covenant which the meal celebrates—water baptism.

Who Should Administer the Lord's Supper?

Since the local church is the only biblically recognized authority responsible for the continuation of the ordinances, the local church is responsible for the administration of the Lord's Supper. Most Southern Baptists have contended that the Supper should not be administered by denominational schools, conferences, conventions, or individuals. Thus, the pastor should not take the Lord's Supper to individuals and administer it personally. Such a practice inevitably will lead to doctrinal error and divisiveness in the church. Further, the matter of "open" or "close" communion logically falls within the jurisdiction and responsibility of the local church.

Normally, the pastor (with the assistance of the deacons) administers the Lord's Supper, but this is not mandatory. As with baptism, the local church has the right to authorize any spiritually qualified person to administer the ordinance. It is a serious responsibility for any local church to administer the ordinances in a biblical and orderly fashion.

How Often Should the Lord's Supper Be Observed?

People often ask, "How frequently should the Lord's Supper be observed?" The Scriptures are not specific at this point. Paul simply said, "As often as ye eat this bread, and drink this cup, ye do shew the Lord's death till he come" (1 Cor. 11:26). The Passover was observed once a year; but the text suggests that the Lord's Supper should be observed more frequently than that. Some churches observe the Supper once a month, some once a quarter, some once a year. Most churches probably observe the Supper once a quarter. First Baptist Church, Dallas, observes the Supper once a month, alternating between the morning and evening services. But the matter of frequency is left to the discretion of the local church.

What Elements Should Be Used?

It is only natural that unleavened bread and unfermented grape juice be used in the observance of the Lord's Supper. The use of these elements symbolizes the sinlessness of Christ (2 Cor. 5:21; Heb. 4:16; 7:26; 1 Pet. 2:22; 1 John 3:5) and are forceful sermons within themselves.

CONCLUSION

Baptists have been so busy talking about who should be excluded from the Lord's table that we have forgotten to insist that all believers should be in regular attendance at the Lord's Supper. In all of my years of ministry I have never been able to understand why some professed believers deliberately shun the Lord's Supper services. The Lord's Supper ought to be one of the most meaningful services in the life of the local church. If it is not, the pastor and the people ought to work together to make it so. "This do . . . in remembrance of me" (1 Cor. 11:25).

Chapter 8

The Future
of the Church

ON EARTH

Potential Expansion

One of the most astonishing things our Lord will ever say to us is what he said prior to his crucifixion and resurrection and consequent departure from earth. In John 14:12 he said, "Verily, verily, I say unto you, He that believeth on me, the works that I do shall he do also; and greater works than these shall he do; because I go unto my Father." The greatest and most phenomenal products of the Christian faith, Jesus said, are yet to come. What the Gospels record are those things that Jesus began to do and teach. The centuries that follow shall witness the expansion of the church, the continuation of Christ's deeds, his actions, his works in the earth as he presides over them in heaven.

In Acts, our Lord himself set the potential and the pattern for the expansion of the body of Christ. Acts 1:8 records that the first disciples were promised unlimited power, "Ye shall receive power, after that the Holy Ghost is come upon you: and ye shall be witnesses unto me . . . ." As a result the evangelization of Judea in the villages, in the highways, and in the byways was launched (Acts 2—7). Expanding further, the gospel was preached in Samaria. The first Christians were primarily Jews, who by nature were antagonistic to Samaritans. However, these Jewish Christians' new nature and new mission sent them to the Samaritans with the gospel. Then a Jew converted out of the Gentile world, the treasurer of Ethiopia under Candace, the queen, received the gospel (Acts 8). Luke then traced the progress of the evangelistic movement to a Gentile who had forsaken his heathen idols, Cornelius, the centurion of the Roman army in Caesarea (Acts 10). Then the gospel reached Antioch, where a local church was established. The mission to the uttermost parts of the earth was initiated from Antioch (Acts 13).

The pattern set in Acts 1:8 is best understood to be a simultaneous one rather than a sequential one. Jesus said, *"Both* in Jerusalem, and in all Judaea, ..."* Even before the evangelism of Jerusalem became extensive, the disciples moved on to Samaria, on to Antioch, on to Corinth, and on to the uttermost parts of the earth simultaneously.

The same should be true of us. When a person becomes a Christian and is filled with the Spirit, witnessing becomes natural. His neighbor knows by his witness that he is a Christian. Both the mailman and the garbage collector hear from him of Jesus through a tract or a personal word. At the grocery store, the meatcutter, as well as the cashier, senses that this person has been with Jesus.

It is impractical to suppose that we can extend our evangelistic enterprise to the uttermost parts of the earth unless we indeed can engage in evangelism in our own backyard.

World Missions

The church has but one primary mission—to make disciples or to lead others to follow Jesus. It is not religious dialogue or political liberation as some persons see it. It is neither the feeding of the hungry nor the clothing of the naked. Nor is it the education of the masses or the advocacy of justice. All the preceding are good and necessary. The needs they represent were not ignored by Jesus, and they must not be ignored by the church. Sensitizing Christians to those needs and equipping Christians to address themselves to those needs is a part of the church's discipling task. The church's identity rests upon her mission to evangelize and to disciple. When these are neglected, the church, any body of local believers, dies by the loss of identity. The salt has lost its flavor and is trodden under foot; the light has lost its brightness and has succumbed to darkness.

In fulfillment of her mission, the church engages in missions—the activities and programs used to lead persons to Christ. Thus, we speak of home missions, of language missions, of missions to the Indians, of the Union Gospel Mission ministering to homeless and jobless people, of churches in their early beginnings as missions.

We also speak of world missions. It is Dallas reaching out to Delhi and Dahomey with the gospel message. It is Texas reaching out to Turkey and Tanzania through persons bearing the gospel message. It is our Southern Baptist denomination probing the ends of the earth for unevangelized peoples and overcoming manmade barriers to present God's life-saving message. Since not all of us can go as missionaries, we send missionaries. Since many churches are too small to fulfill their world mission, we join hands in the Cooperative Program. We give to an Annie Armstrong Easter Offering for home missions and to the Lottie Moon Christmas Offering for world missions. We have the biggest missionary giving and outreach program administered by our Foreign Mission Board. And most important, Southern Baptists are engaged in Bold Mission Thrust—an impressive goal of taking the gospel to every living person by the year 2000.

Indeed, as Christ declared, we shall do greater things than the Lord ever accomplished in his earthly ministry. The church has men like Billy Graham, who has addressed more people than were converted during the first century. We have churches with multifaceted ministries extending the gospel invitation to all levels of society. We have missionaries in almost every area of the world. We have the wonder of satellite telecommunications and other technological means to spread the gospel more effectively and more extensively than ever before. But let us not forget, we "shall receive power, after that the Holy Ghost is come . . ." (Acts 1:8).

"The field is the world," Jesus said (Matt. 13:38). Thus far, we have not covered the world; there is yet more to evangelize. But Southern Baptists have, after 130 years, established work in 94 nations. Bold Mission Thrust has challenged us to reach the whole world before the end of this century. That calls for neighborhood as well as world witness. Despite the record numbers of missionary appointments at present, we are still able to fill only one-fifth of the requests for personnel. Not all are called for service in the world missions corps. But it is also a grim truth that not all who are called to world missions are serving the purpose of that call. It involves a sacrifice.

The church's pioneer potential is limitless; our victorious assault is secured. We shall receive power and be witnesses. And when the church assaults the forces of hell with the gospel message, no amount of force can stop it; no power of earth can subdue it. We are more than conquerors through Christ. Look out world! The church is coming with a message for you!

> At the sign of triumph Satan's host doth flee;
> On, then, Christian soldiers, On to victory!
> Hell's foundations quiver At the shout of praise;
> Brothers, lift your voices, Loud your anthems raise!
> Onward, Christian soldiers, Marching as to war,
> With the cross of Jesus Going on before!
>
> Sabine Baring-Gould, 1864

PERSONAL LEARNING ACTIVITY 21
As a part of the church, you share in the church's responsibility and challenge to fulfill the mission of Christ. List ways that you can be directly, personally involved in your church's witness and ministry. Then examine *The Commission, Home Missions, Brotherhood Builder,* and other mission periodicals to discover how you and your church are involved beyond your community in fulfilling Christ's mission.

IN HEAVEN
Although Baptists hold that there is but one people of God throughout history, they also insist on the uniqueness and dis-

tinctiveness of the church, the body of Christ. The truth about that body is a mystery—a truth previously hidden but in God's own time revealed to men (Eph. 3:5). There was no church apart from the glorification of Christ and apart from the coming of the Holy Spirit. Before there was a church, there was no body into which the Spirit baptizes (1 Cor. 12:13). The experience of the permanent indwelling of the Holy Spirit was not the common experience of believers before the church existed. So, we say that within that general category of the people of God, the church is a distinct entity.

Christ's Return for the Church

Building upon the analogy of marriage, the future of the church begins at the coming of the Bridegroom for the bride. Oriental marriage customs shed light on this beautiful imagery. The custom comes in three different tenses. First, the pair enters a legal contract sealed by a dowry or a purchase price given by the groom to the bride's father. Likewise, Christ, the divine Bridegroom, purchased the church, his bride, with his blood (Acts 20:28). Having accomplished this stage, the Oriental couple is betrothed. This is not simply a promise to marry as in modern-day engagements; it is the initiation of marriage, without physical union. Having been purchased, the church is *now* the bride of Christ (2 Cor. 11:2).

The second step in the Oriental marriage is the procession to the bride's home, led by the groom. He is accompanied by his friends and relatives and is guided by torches. The bride watches and is ready for that moment (Matt. 25). The church as the bride of Christ awaits the coming of the Bridegroom to get his bride. Jesus promised to come for the bride. His promise was so sure that although it was future when he said it, he spoke of it as though it were a present reality (John 14:3). Paul described this experience as being caught up to meet the Lord in the air and being with him forever (1 Thess. 4:17).

Then the third stage takes place. After the bride and groom arrive at their future home, the marriage supper or feast begins. It was at a similar occasion that Jesus changed the water into wine at Cana (John 2). The apostle John depicted this scene as he saw it take place by revelation (Rev. 19:7-9).

Bride, get yourself ready; your redemption is drawing nigh. He is coming soon, and it may be morning, night, or noon.

The Church and the Judgment Seat of Christ
The clear teaching of the Scriptures is that the believer "shall not come into condemnation; but is passed from death unto life" (John 5:24). The judgment that we talk about is not to determine whether the believer is saved but for the giving of rewards. As a result of this judgment, some will be rewarded richly. Others will barely pass the test but nevertheless will be saved "yet so as by fire" (1 Cor. 3:15).

The Church and Her Rewards
We shall be rewarded for the services we render to the cause of Christ. Those rewards will be given according to how faithfully we have used the talents/possessions God committed to us.

PERSONAL LEARNING ACTIVITY 22
The Bible mentions several crowns that will be given as rewards. Beside each reference, write the crown identified in that verse.
1 Thessalonians 2:19 _____
2 Timothy 4:8 _____
James 1:12 _____
1 Peter 5:4 _____
1 Corinthians 9:25 _____

The Bible also states that the church worshiping in heaven will cast their crowns before the Lamb as an act of worship (Rev. 4:4,10).

The Church and Her Heavenly Home
"If in this life only we have hope in Christ, we are of all men most miserable" (1 Cor. 15:19). The best is yet to come for the body of Christ. We look forward to being with Christ forever in

heaven. Three heavens are alluded to in the Scriptures: (1) the firmament (Gen. 1:8), referring to the earth's atmosphere; (2) the stellar universe, the sun, moon, and stars, and so on (Ps. 19:1); and (3) the unique dwelling place of God (Heb. 4:14). The unique dwelling place of God is that with which we are concerned. Heaven is a place where God will abide with his people; and it is described in Revelation 21 as a place void of sorrow, death, pain, and other travails of the present life (v. 4), a place of immaculate beauty (vv. 9-26), a place free from sin and defilement (v. 27), a condition of perpetual life (Rev. 22:1-2), and a place of God's eternal dominion (Rev. 22:5).

Heaven will be more than the superlatives of human language and imagination could describe. It is one of those things beyond human description which God has reserved for those who love him (1 Cor. 2:9). Heaven is a place of activity and responsibility, where we shall worship and reign with God forever (Rev. 22:5).

No institution is more beloved of God than the church. No future is more glorious than the church's future. No present activity is more rewarding and more optimistic than the church's fulfillment of her mission. Given the opportunity to choose between being the President of the United States or some other world-renowned leader, I would rather be a pastor of a church. To paraphrase Edgar A. Guest's "House by the Side of the Road":

> Let me have my church on a downtown street
>   Where the race of men go by;
> The men who are good; the men who are bad
>   As good and as bad as I.
> I would not sit in the scorner's seat,
>   Or hurl the cynics ban,
> Let me have my church on Ervay Street
>   And be a friend of man.

FOR FURTHER STUDY

If you feel a need for further study in some of the areas dealt with in this chapter, you will find the Equipping Center module *How to Start New Work* to be an excellent resource.

Clyde Denton Jr.

Use these group study guides to provide the kind of group setting and group experience that will enable this study to come to life in the lives of group members.

Small-Group Study Guides

Bill Latham

Session 1
WHAT IS THIS THING CALLED CHURCH?
Chapters 1 and 3

Training goal: At the end of this session, each person should be able to demonstrate his understanding of the church by
- defining the church in generic, relational, and functional terms;
- listing four characteristics that have typified the church through the centuries;
- assessing the degree to which his church feels the influence of rival forces;
- listing and applying to his own church four factors that have kept the church viable through the centuries.

Before the Session
- Get copies of *The Doctrine of the Church* to distribute at the session to members who have not received copies already.
- Have the following materials on hand for use in the session: material for making name tags, hymnals, pencils and paper, extra Bibles, and a chalkboard or sheets of newsprint.
- Select a responsive reading for use during the session.
- Prepare a theme chart and an arrow as illustrated or use kit item 1 mounted on a cardboard backing.

THE DOCTRINE OF THE CHURCH

Session 1
What Is This Thing Called Church?

Session 2
The Church: Its Roots and Branches

Session 3
The Church's Open Secret

Session 4
The Remembrance and the Witness

Session 5
Commitment to the Body

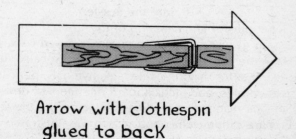

Arrow with clothespin glued to back

• Check with the person who keeps your church's Church Study Course records to learn which members will complete the requirements for the Baptist Doctrine Diploma upon completion of this study.

• Prepare three charts as illustrated on page 118 or use kit items 2-4.

• Use the following exercises to prepare work sheets for use by members. Use 8½ by 11 sheets and leave ample writing space to complete the exercises. Kit item 5 is a master you can use to make these work sheets.

Exercise 1
In what sense is the word *church* a generic term?

In what sense is the word *church* a relational term?

In what sense is the word *church* a functional term?

Exercise 2
The four characteristics that have typified the church through the centuries are: (1) D_____,
(2) D_____ , (3) D_____,
and (4) I_____.

Exercise 3
Four factors that have kept the church viable are:
(1) a P_____ H_____
for G_____ , (2) the
A_____ N_____ of the
S_____, (3) the P_____
N_____ of the C_____,
and (4) the H_____ of its A_____ .

Circle the factor that is most in evidence in your church.

What could be done to strengthen the influence of the other factors in your church?

CHARACTERISTICS THAT HAVE TYPIFIED THE CHURCH

Division   Dilution

Declaration   Triumph

FACTORS IN THE CHURCH'S VIABILITY

Perpetual hunger for God
Arresting nature of the Scriptures
Permeating nature of the church
Heroism of its adherents

RIVAL CLAIMS

Cults
Materialism
Humanistic philosophy
Parachurch organizations

Exercise 4

Four rival claims that affect the church today are:

(1) C_____ , (2) M_____ ,

(3) H_____ P_____ , and

(4) P_____ O_____ .

Circle the claim that has had the greatest effect on your church. Why do you think the claim has affected your church?

What can your church do to counter that claim?

During the Session

Getting Started

• As members arrive, register each person, distribute copies of *The Doctrine of the Church,* and ask each person to prepare a name tag.

• If members do not already know one another, spend a few minutes becoming acquainted.

• Explain how study course credit can be earned for this study. Explain the Baptist Doctrine Diploma and the study requirements for earning that diploma (see pp. 140-42). Ask how many members have already earned credits that will count toward this diploma. Recognize any persons who will complete requirements for the diploma at the end of this study. Urge members to schedule individual studies of other books to complete requirements for the diploma.

• Distribute hymnals and lead the group in singing "The Church's One Foundation." Ask that as members sing, they consider the words to discover one significant statement the hymn makes about the church.

• Lead members in a responsive reading that deals with the church. Ask that as they read, they consider the words to discover one significant statement made about the church. (An index of readings is at the back of most hymnals.)

• Ask members to suggest significant statements about the church that were either read or sung. List these on the chalkboard or on newsprint fastened to the wall. Then ask members to tell how they hope to benefit from this study and what are some of their questions about the church they would like to have answered. Write these responses on the chalkboard or on newsprint.

• Lead in prayer, expressing thanks for the church. Ask God to bless the study and use it to deepen each person's understanding of and commitment to the church.

• Use the theme chart and the information in Introduction in the text to introduce and overview the study. State the training goal for each session and mention some of the learning activities that will be used. Stress the importance of members' bringing their Bibles to each session and studying the assigned chapters in the text before each session.

• Clip the arrow to the theme chart so that it points to the title for session 1. Ask, What is your answer to the question? Allow time for responses. Then distribute pencils and paper and ask each person to write his own preliminary definition of the word *church*.

Studying the Bible
Resources for this session's Bible study are under "Descriptive Terminology" in chapter 3 of the text.

• State that the word *church* can be defined in generic, relational, and functional terms. Lend Bibles to members who did not bring their own. Ask members to take careful notes as you lead the Bible study.

• Divide the chalkboard into three columns or fasten three pieces of newsprint to the wall. Label the columns or sheets *generic*, *relational*, and *functional*.

• Under *generic*, write *ekklesia* and lead a study of appropriate Scripture passages to show how *church* is a generic term. As each passage is studied, write the reference on the chalkboard or on the newsprint.

• Under *relational*, write *bride of Christ* and follow the same Bible study procedure to show how this term describes the church in terms of the Christian's relation to Christ.

• Under *relational*, write *fellowship*. Follow the same Bible study procedure to show how this term describes the church in terms of the relationship between Christians.

● Under *relational*, write *functional*. Follow the same Bible study procedure to show how this term speaks of the church in terms of the relationship between Christians and between Christians and Christ.

● Under *functional*, write *kingdom of priests*. Follow the same Bible study procedure to show how this term describes the church in terms of what the church should be and do.

Considering

● Give members five minutes to review chapter 1 in the text.

● Ask members to recall the four characteristics that have typified the church through the centuries. After the characteristics are recalled, display the prepared chart and lead members to discuss the characteristics.

● Ask members to recall the four factors that have kept the church viable through the centuries. After the factors are recalled, display the prepared chart and lead a brief discussion of the factors.

● Ask members to recall the four rival claims that affect the church today. After the claims are recalled, display the prepared chart. Lead a brief discussion of the claims and how their influence has affected your church.

Applying

● Form four work teams and give each person a work sheet. Assign a different exercise on the work sheet to each team.

● After a brief work period, call for reports and lead a brief discussion of each report.

Concluding

● Ask members to complete the work sheet before coming to the next session and to rework their preliminary definitions of the church.

● Assign chapters 2 and 4 in the text for the next session. Encourage members to complete the personal learning activities in the text as a part of their study.

● Close with prayer, thanking God for what the church has been through the centuries and for what your church is today.

Session 2
THE CHURCH: ITS ROOTS AND BRANCHES
Chapters 2 and 4

Training goal: At the end of this session, each person should be able to demonstrate his understanding of the origin and the mission of the church by

- drawing and explaining a diagram that presents visually the church's origin and mission;
- using that understanding to evaluate his own church's ministry.

Before the Session

- Display the theme chart.
- Have a chalkboard or sheets of newsprint available.
- Have pencils and paper available.
- Prepare the Bible study chart as shown or use kit item 6.
- Prepare completion statement sheets for use by members or use kit item 7. At the top of the sheet, write these instructions: *Write a sentence or two to complete each statement so that it best reflects your personal feelings or judgments. Be as honest as possible. You will not have to share what you have written unless you wish to.* Use these completion statements on the sheets. Leave ample writing space between each incomplete statement.

   1. When I think of my church as Christ himself extending his mission into today's world, I feel

   2. My church is most effective in extending and fulfilling the mission of Christ when it

   3. The area in which my church is weakest in extending and fulfilling the mission of Christ is

   4. When I realize that the Holy Spirit has given me gifts that the church needs for extending and fulfilling the mission of Christ, I feel

5. The gift that I use most effectively is

6. The gift that I have but may not be using as effectively as I could is

• Enlist your minister of education or other leaders in your church to be prepared to explain the meanings of evangelism, worship, teaching, and nurture and to explain how your church involves members in each of these functions. This presentation should stress also the fact that the church is dependent on the gifts given each member by the Holy Spirit if the mission of Christ is to be fulfilled. Resources for this presentation are "The Fulfillment of the Mission of Christ by the Church" in chapter 4 of the text and "Pentecost as Endowment for the Church" in chapter 2.

During the Session
Getting Started
• Welcome and register any new members.
• Lead the group in singing "To Worship, Work, and Witness" or "Rise Up, O Men of God."
• Clip the arrow to the theme chart so that it points to the title of this session.
• Lead in prayer, thanking God for the heritage of the church and asking that your church will be directed and empowered to be and to do all that it should.

Studying the Bible
• Display the Bible study chart for this session and explain that the church's origin and mission can be pictured as the roots, the trunk, and the branches of a tree.
• Write *Old Testament concepts* on the left root and say, One part of the church's origin is rooted in the Old Testament concept of God's purpose for his people. To help members understand this concept, lead a study and discussion of one or more of the Scripture passages listed in personal learning activity 4. Use one or more of the Scripture passages listed in personal learning activity 5 to help members see the similarity

between the ethical requirements placed on Israel and those placed on the church.

● Write *concept of the kingdom* on the right root and say, Another part of the church's origin is rooted in the concept of the kingdom of God. Use material under "The Kingdom of God and the Church" in chapter 2 of the text to help members understand the implications of Matthew 4:17 and Mark 1:14-15.

● On the three parts of the central root, write *Jesus, Pentecost,* and *Scripture.* Lead a study and discussion of passages you have selected from "Jesus and the Church" in chapter 2 of the text.

Considering

● Ask members to recall what the text stated to be the mission of the church. (*To extend the mission of Christ.*) Write *mission of Christ* on the trunk of the tree.

● Allow five minutes for each person to review the section "The Redemptive Mission of Christ" in chapter 4 of the text. Ask each person to underline in his book one key idea in each division of that section. After the review period, ask members to share with the group the ideas they underlined. As each idea is shared, write it on the chalkboard or on pieces of newsprint fastened to the wall.

● After the brainstorming is completed, allow members to ask questions and discuss the ideas that have been suggested.

● Point to the ideas that have been written and say, If these are the characteristics of Christ's mission, and if the church is to be an extension of that mission, what do these things we have written say to the church? (*These will be the characteristics of a church that is extending effectively the mission of Christ.*)

● The text discusses four ways the church should function to extend the mission of Christ. Ask members to recall these functions. (*evangelism, worship, teaching, nurture*) As these are recalled, write the terms on the branches of the tree.

● Call on the minister of education or other leaders enlisted to explain the meaning of these terms and to discuss with the group how your church involves members in each of these functions.

Applying

• Take down the Bible study chart and distribute pencils and completion-statement sheets to members. Ask each person to use the back of his sheet to sketch some visual presentation of the origin and mission of the church. Explain that members may reproduce the Bible study chart or they may devise a different one. The important thing is to show the relationship of the concepts that were dealt with in the Bible study. After each person has completed his sketch, he should write a sentence or two to complete each statement on his sheet.

• After a few minutes of work time, ask if any members devised a different visual presentation of the origin and the mission of the church. Ask that these be shown and explained to the group. Then ask volunteers to share and discuss with the group the way they completed some of the statements.

Concluding

• Assign chapter 5 in the text for the next session.
• Make advance assignments for the next session.
• Ask members to sit with heads bowed and meditate on the fact that theirs is the responsibility of fulfilling the mission of Christ in the world today. Then lead in prayer, asking that each person be empowered to respond to life situations as Christ himself would respond.

Session 3
THE CHURCH'S OPEN SECRET
Chapter 5

Training goal: At the end of this session, each person should be able to
- list the leaders of a New Testament church and explain the responsibilities of each;
- explain how members of the body relate to leaders in the work of the church.

Before the Session

• Enlist one member to summarize the information under "The Historic Forms of Church Government" in chapter 5 of the text.

Ask this person to prepare a chart that presents visually what he will say in his summary or give him kit item 8.

• Have hymnals available for use.

• Have pencils and paper to distribute to members.

• Prepare the Bible study chart as illustrated on page 128.

• Prepare a work sheet for use by members as illustrated on page 129. Use 8½ by 11 sheets and leave ample writing space. Kit item 9 is a master you can use to make copies of this work sheet.

• If possible, enlist your pastor to lead the Bible study for this session. Provide him with a copy of the text, the work sheet for this session, and the Bible study chart for this session. Suggest that he follow the teaching plan suggested here, but leave him free to develop the study differently if he wishes. Request that he take care to cover information that members will need for completing the work sheet later in the session.

During the Session

Getting Started

• Distribute pencils and paper as members arrive.

• Lead the group in singing "I Would Be True" or "We Are Called to Be God's People."

• Lead in prayer, asking that each member of the body will be committed to helping the body function as it should.

• Lead the group in a word-association exercise. Explain that you are going to call out some words and each person is to write the first thing that comes to mind. Emphasize the importance of not taking time to think but of writing the *first thought that comes to mind*. Then call out these words: *pastor, bishop, elder, deacon, minister.* After the exercise, ask several volunteers to share what they wrote.

• Call attention to the theme chart and ask, Does the title of this session stir your curiosity? Then ask members to recall the central idea of the previous session. (*The church is to extend and fulfill the mission of Christ.*) Make a brief introductory

PASTOR
poimen

ELDER
presbuteros

BISHOP
episkopos

DEACON
diakonos

MINISTER
diakonos

Shepherd

Providing
whatever is
needed

A respected and
trusted leader

One who loves
and cares

Providing
whatever is
needed

PASTOR
poimen
Ephesians 4:11

The root meaning of this word is

The role implied in this term is

Ways my pastor fills this role are

ELDER
presbuteros
1 Timothy 5:17-19; Titus 1:5-9

The root meaning of this word is

The role implied in this term is

Ways my pastor fills this role are

BISHOP
episkopos
Titus 1:5-9; 1 Timothy 3:1-7

The root meaning of this word is

The role implied in this term is

Ways my pastor fills this role are

DEACON
diakonos
Acts 6:1-6; 1 Timothy 3:8-13

The root meaning of this word is

The role implied in this term is

Ways my deacons fill this role are

MINISTER
diakonos
Ephesians 4:11-12; 1 Corinthians 3:6; 6:4

The root meaning of this word is

Ways I fill this role are

Use the back of the sheet to answer.

statement to the effect that fulfilling the mission of Christ is an overwhelming task and a seemingly impossible one. Yet, if it were completely out of the realm of possibility, Christ would not have charged us with the responsibility. So, there must be some secret not evident to the mind of man for achieving the task. The church is charged with the responsibility and also is told the means of carrying out the responsibility. This open secret is evident to those whose eyes have been opened by the Holy Spirit to the truth of the Scriptures. Fulfilling the mission of Christ becomes possible when every member of Christ's body functions and relates properly to the other members.

• State training goal for this session.
• State that a part of the church's open secret is the way the members of the church do the work of the church by working together in a harmonious and Spirit-led unity. This is reflected in the form of government used in Baptist churches.
• Call on the person enlisted in advance to summarize the information under "The Historic Forms of Church Government" in chapter 5 of the text.
• State that another part of the church's open secret is the way leaders and members relate to one another to do the work of the church.

Studying the Bible
As you lead the Bible study, you should be aware of the information members will need to complete the work-sheet exercise at the end of the session.

• Fasten the Bible study chart to the wall and fasten the five flash cards beside it. Ask members if they encountered any new or surprising ideas as they studied the meanings of these terms in the text. Allow time for responses. Ask, Which flash card is most appropriate with the word *pastor*? (*Shepherd*) After members have responded, fasten the flash card to the chart in the space below *pastor*. Lead a study of Ephesians 4:11 and any other passages you may select to help members understand the role described by this term.
• Ask, Which flash card is most appropriate with the word *elder*? (*A respected and trusted leader*) Lead a study of

1 Timothy 5:17-19; Titus 1:5-9, and other passages you may select to help members understand this term.

• Ask, Which flash card is most appropriate with the word *bishop*? (*One who loves and cares*) Lead a study of Titus 5:1-9; 1 Timothy 3:1-7, and other passages you may select to help members understand the meaning of this term.

• Ask, Which flash card is most appropriate with the word *deacon*? (*Providing whatever is needed*) Lead a study of Acts 6:1-6; 1 Timothy 3:8-13, and other passages you may select to help members understand the meaning of this term.

• Place the final flash card in place and ask, Were you surprised to learn in your study that the words *deacon* and *minister* both come from the same Greek word (*diakonos*)? Lead a study of Ephesians 4:11-12; 1 Corinthians 3:6; 6:4 to help members understand that each Christian is to serve by providing what is necessary to meet the needs of others. Every Christian is a minister. Also, use the Ephesians passage to help members understand that the function of the pastor is to equip members of the church to be ministers.

Considering
Use the following questions to lead members to discuss the ideas presented in the Bible study.

• How did you react to the idea that your pastor is also a bishop and an elder?

• How do you react to the writer's statement that a deacon's responsibility is to "supply the need" rather than to serve on a "managerial board"?

• How do you react to the idea that you are our church's ministers?

• How would it affect our church if we considered only the pastor to be a minister?

Applying
• Distribute the work sheet for this session and ask members to work individually to complete it.

• After a brief work period, ask members to compare and discuss the way they completed their work sheets.

Concluding
- Make advance assignments for next session.
- Ask some group members to assist you in checking on persons who registered in the first two sessions but failed to return.
- Assign chapters 6 and 7 in the text for the next session.

Session 4
THE REMEMBRANCE AND THE WITNESS
Chapters 6-7

Training goal: At the end of this session, each person should be able to demonstrate his understanding of baptism and the Lord's Supper by
- explaining the symbolism of each;
- determining and explaining an appropriate course of action to be taken in a series of case studies.

Before the Session
- Have hymnals available for the session.
- Display the unit aid with the arrow pointing to the title of this session.
- Enlist a person to give a brief review of the section titled "Practical Considerations About the Lord's Supper" in chapter 7 of the text.
- Enlist several persons to give testimonies about their baptisms. Try to enlist persons whose testimonies would be unusual, such as a person who was baptized out of doors, a person who was first baptized in another denomination, a person who has been a Christian for many years, a person who has been a Christian a very short time, and so on.
- Write the following case studies on separate cards or use kit item 10.

Case Study 1
John and Mark participate regularly in their church's Thursday night visitation. On this particular Thursday night their assignment is to visit a family who recently purchased a small farm a few miles from the church. Early in their visit John and Mark discover that the mother and two children are members of a

Baptist church in the community they moved from. The father is not a Christian. After several hours of prayerful, loving witnessing, John and Mark lead the father to trust Christ. The father relates how as a child he heard his preacher preach that a person would go to hell if he died without being baptized. He asks John and Mark to take him at once to a small pond on the farm and baptize him. What should John and Mark do?

Case Study 2
Since their church does not provide for children over three years of age, Dan and Mary recently began taking their four-year-old daughter, Erin, to the worship services. On this particular morning the church observed the Lord's Supper. Erin brightened immediately and was intensely attentive to what the pastor and the deacons were doing. When the juice and bread were distributed, Erin became very upset when she was not permitted to participate. She later explained to her parents that she had always had juice and cookies with the boys and girls in the nursery and she was hurt and confused when the grownups would not share their juice and cookies with her. What should Dan and Mary do?

Case Study 3
Ronald is in his first year at the largest university in the state. Recently he began participating in a campus prayer and fellowship group. On this particular evening the study centers around the meaning of the Lord's Supper. At the conclusion of the study, the leader opens a bag, takes out bread and juice, and suggests that the group join in observing the Lord's Supper. What should Ronald do?

Case Study 4
During the invitation hymn Aaron Leech presented himself for membership in Fellowship Baptist Church. His statement is that in his younger years he had made a profession of faith and had been immersed into the membership of a nondenominational church. What action should Fellowship Baptist Church take?

● Prepare a Bible study chart for this session or use kit item 11. Use several sheets of newsprint to write 1 Corinthians 11:18-29. Leave space to make notes later at the edges of the sheets.

During the Session
Getting Started
● Lead the group in singing "Here at Thy Table, Lord" and then lead in prayer, thanking God for the eternal truths that baptism and the Lord's Supper symbolize.
● Call attention to the theme chart and state the subject of this session's study. Then introduce the persons enlisted to

give testimonies.
• State that the purpose of this session is to help members gain a deeper understanding of baptism and the Lord's Supper, and state the session training goal.

Studying the Bible
• Lead a study of Romans 6:1-13 to help members understand the threefold symbolism of baptism. "The Meaning of Baptism" in chapter 6 of the text is a resource for this study.
• Fasten this session's Bible study chart to the wall and lead a study of 1 Corinthians 11:18-29. As you lead the study, mark and label appropriate words and phrases on the chart. Ask members to refer to the way they marked this same passage of Scripture at the beginning of chapter 7 in the text. "The Meaning of the Lord's Supper" in chapter 7 of the text is a resource for this part of the study.

Considering
• Ask members to work together to review and to discuss the way they completed personal learning activity 16. Let this discussion surface any misunderstandings or incomplete understandings members may have about the meaning, the mode, the candidate, the authority, or the purpose in baptism. Don't be satisfied simply to identify correct responses to the questions. Lead members to discuss why each possible answer is either right or wrong. Doing this will review and reinforce material covered in the Bible study and other material members have studied in the text.
• Call on the person enlisted to review the section "Practical Considerations About the Lord's Supper" in chapter 7.

Applying
• Form four discussion groups and give one of the prepared case studies to each group with instruction to be prepared to report to the group in five minutes.
• After the discussion time, ask each group to read its case study and report how it would have handled the situation. Allow time for discussion and questions after each report.

Concluding
- Assign chapter 8 in the text for the next session.
- Lead in prayer, thanking God that we have been given the remembrance and the witness of the Lord's Supper and baptism.

Session 5
COMMITMENT TO THE BODY
Chapter 8

Training goal: At the end of this session, each person should demonstrate a deeper commitment to the church by
- having identified areas where his commitment is highest and most effective;
- having outlined and being committed to a definite plan to give the church the maximum benefit of his strongest and most effective commitments;
- having identified areas where his commitment is lowest and least effective;
- having identified factors that have reduced the level or the effectiveness of his commitment in those areas;
- having outlined and by being committed to a definite plan for increasing the level and the effectiveness of his commitment in those areas.

Before the Session
- Have hymnals available for the session.
- Display the theme chart.
- Enlist the church media center director (librarian) to bring to the session and to offer to check out to members books that can be studied toward meeting requirements for the Baptist Doctrine Diploma.
- Enlist as a panel the pastor and the leaders of the program organizations of the church. Give them copies of the questions to be discussed so they can give adequate thought to their answers. Impress on panel members that this will be an oppor-

Areas in which my commitment is highest and most effective are:

Areas in which my commitment is lowest and least effective are:

Steps I will take to give my church maximum benefit from this commitment are:

Steps I will take to deepen my sense of commitment in these areas are:

tunity to lead those who have been in this study to a deeper commitment to the body of Christ. Explain that it is to be a session in which members engage in self-evaluation and set definite plans for deepening their commitment and involvement. All this will be done off what panel members say in their discussion. Urge panel members to pray earnestly about this time they will spend with the group. Plan to meet with the panel before the session for a time of prayer.

• Arrange at the front of the meeting room a table and chairs for the panel.

• Prepare a work sheet for this session as illustrated. Kit item 12 is a master you can use to make these work sheets.

During the Session

Getting Started

• Lead the group in singing "Onward, Christian Soldiers" and lead in prayer, thanking God for the participation of members in this study and asking God's special direction in this session.

• Use the theme chart to lead a brief review of the study. Ask members to recall and to state briefly the main ideas that were developed in each session.

• State the training goal for this session and explain that the purpose of this session is to help members make definite plans for putting into action in their lives some of the truths they have learned about the church.

Studying the Bible

• Lead a study of John 14:9-14 to help members understand how the church expanded the things that Jesus began to do and to teach.

• Use selected passages from Acts to trace the expansion of the church in the New Testament period.

• Lead a study of 1 Corinthians 3:9-15 and the passages listed in personal learning activity 22 to help members to realize their accountability for being responsible members of the body of Christ and to identify the characteristics that will be rewarded by God.

Considering

• Introduce the panel and ask that as members listen to the panel discussion they be thinking about the points at which their commitment to the church is strongest and most effective and the points at which it is lowest and least effective. Use the following questions to moderate the panel discussion.

—At what points in the life of our church (worship, Bible study, training, missions organizations, ministry, witnessing, fellowship, nurture, and so on) do the members seem to have the strongest sense of commitment? Why do you think this is true?

—What can the church do to receive maximum benefit from this strong sense of commitment?

—What could members of this group begin doing immediately to use to great advantage the commitments they feel to the church and to one another?

—At what points in the life of our church (worship, Bible study, training, missions organizations, ministry, witnessing, fellowship, nurture, and so on) do the members seem to have the lowest sense of commitment? Why do you think this is true?

—What can the church do to deepen members' sense of commitment to these areas of our church's life?

—What could members of this group begin doing immediately to deepen their commitment to the church and to one another?

• After the panel discussion, allow a brief period for members to ask questions and to discuss what panelists have said.

Applying

• Distribute the work sheet for this session and ask each person to work individually to complete his. Assure members that the work done on the work sheet is private and any sharing of work will be voluntary. Ask each person to have a brief, private quiet time before beginning. Suggest that for his quiet time each person read Ephesians 4:11-16 and pray.

• After the individual work time, allow volunteers to share whatever they wish from their self-evaluations and their plans.

Concluding

• Explain once more the requirements for receiving the Baptist Doctrine Diploma (see ses. 1). Call on the church media library director to show and to offer to check out to members additional books or Equipping Center modules for study toward the diploma.

• Give make-up assignments to members for any sessions missed. (Don't overlook members who may be absent from this session.)

• Lead members to review the suggestions for further study at the end of most chapters in the text. Lead them to consider group study or individual study in areas that interest them.

• Lead the group in singing "Take My Life, and Let It Be." Lead a prayer of commitment to the body of Christ.

After the Session

• Use the Church Study Course Credit Request form to request credit for all members who qualify.

• Return all unused materials to the resource kit. Gather all unused texts and return them and the resource kit to the church media library or to the place such materials are stored.

• Before storing the resource kit, make a notation on its front that some of its materials have been used in a previous study. A new kit should be ordered for the next study. This kit should be used to supplement the contents of the new kit.

The Church Study Course

The Church Study Course consists of a variety of short-term credit courses for adults and youth and noncredit foundational units for children and preschoolers. The materials are for use in addition to the study and training curriculums made available to the churches on an ongoing basis.

Study courses and foundational units are organized into a system that is promoted by the Sunday School Board, 127 Ninth Avenue, North, Nashville, Tennessee 37234; by the Woman's Missionary Union, 600 North Twentieth Street, Birmingham, Alabama 35203; by the Brotherhood Commission, 1548 Poplar Avenue, Memphis, Tennessee 38104; and by the respective departments of the state conventions affiliated with the Southern Baptist Convention.

Study course materials are flexible enough to be adapted to the needs of any Baptist church. The resources are published in several different formats—textbooks of various sizes, workbooks, kits, and modules. Each item contains an explanation of the Church Study Course.

How to Request Credit for This Course

This book is the text for a course in the subject area Baptist Doctrine. This course is designed for five hours of group study. Credit is awarded for attending class sessions and reading the book. A person who is absent from one or more class sessions must complete the personal learning activities for the material missed.

Credit also is allowed for use of this material in individual study and, if so designated, in lesson course study and in institutional study.

A person desiring credit for individual study should read this book and complete the personal learning activities.

Credit for this study can be applied to one or more diplomas in the Church Study Course.

After the course is completed, the teacher, the study course clerk, the learner, or any person designated by the church should complete Form 151 (Church Study Course Credit Request, Revised 1975) and send it to the Awards Office, 127 Ninth Avenue, North, Nashville, Tennessee 37234. Individuals also may request credit by writing the Awards Office or by using the special coupon in this book.

Reading the book is required for study course credit.

Baptist Doctrine Diploma
The Church Study Course now offers special recognition for study concentrated in the area of Baptist doctrine. The Baptist Doctrine Diploma can be earned by earning credit for the study of the following books.

The Baptist Faith and Message or These Things We Believe
The Doctrine of God
The Doctrine of Man
The Doctrine of Salvation
The Biblical Basis of Missions
An elective in the area of Baptist Doctrine (This book is such an elective.)

Types of Study and Credit
Adults and youth can earn study course credit through individual or group study. Teachers of courses or of foundational units are eligible to receive credit.

1. Class experience.—Group involvement with course material for the designated number of hours for the particular course. Study course credit requirements call for a person to

read, view, or listen to the course material and to attend class sessions. A person who is absent from one or more sessions must complete the personal learning activities or other requirements for the material missed.

2. *Individual study.*—This includes reading, viewing, or listening to course material and completing the specified requirements for the course.

3. *Lesson course study.*—Parallel use of designated study course material during the study of selected units in Church Program Organization periodical curriculum units. Guidance for credit appears in the selected periodical.

4. *Institutional study.*—Parallel use of designated study course material during regular courses at educational institutions, including Seminary Extension Department courses. Guidance for this means of credit is provided by the teacher.

When credit is issued to a person on request, the Awards Office sends two copies of a notice of credit earned to the church. The original copy of the credit slip should be filed by the study course clerk in the participant's record of training folder. The duplicate should be given to the person who earned the credit. Accumulated credits are applied toward a specific leadership diploma or other diplomas in the Church Study Course system.

Detailed information about the Church Study Course system of credits, diplomas, and record keeping is available from the participating agencies. Study course materials, supplementary teaching or learning aids, and forms for record keeping may be ordered from Baptist Book Stores.

The Church Study Course Curriculum
Credit is granted on those courses listed in the current copy of Church Services and Materials Catalog and Church Study Course Catalog. When selecting courses or foundational units, the current catalogs should be checked to determine what study course materials are valid.

INSTRUCTIONS: If requested by the teacher, fill in this form and give it to him when the course is completed. If preferred, mail this request for course credit to

AWARDS OFFICE
THE SUNDAY SCHOOL BOARD, SBC
127 NINTH AVENUE, NORTH
NASHVILLE, TENNESSEE 37234

	State Convention	Association		Indicate Type of Study (X)	Educational
				☐ Class ☐ Individual ☐ Lesson Course ☐ Institution	

CHURCH

Church Name
Mailing Address
City, State, Zip Code

MAIL TO

Mail to (If Different from Church Address)

Street, Route, or P.O. Box

City, State, Zip Code

LAST NAME	FIRST NAME AND MIDDLE INITIAL	MRS. (X)	COURSE TITLE
			The Doctrine of the Church